Climate and Energy Politics in Poland

Climate and Energy Politics in Poland: Debating Carbon Dioxide and Shale Gas presents a new, object-oriented perspective on the challenge faced by Poland, the largest post-socialist EU member state from Central and Eastern Europe (CEE), to produce knowledge about its energy system in the context of climate change.

Drawing on data from five different research projects and two hundred interviews, Lis reflects on how EU accession forced Poland to mobilize their resources and produce expertise on carbon dioxide and shale gas, in order to actively participate in the debates around EU climate change ambitions and goals. A significant lack of capacity and expert institutions made it difficult for Poland to quickly assess the impacts of EU legislation or to propose new solutions for itself, and it is precisely this struggle for knowledge production that will be examined during the course of the book.

This book will be of great interest to students and scholars of energy and resource politics, climate change, EU environmental policy and CEE studies more broadly.

Aleksandra Lis works as Associate Professor at the Adam Mickiewicz University in Poznań, Poland. She holds a PhD from the Central European University in Budapest and has worked as a research fellow at various research institutions and think tanks, including the Center for Science, Technology, Medicine & Society at the University of California, Berkeley; the Center on Organizational Innovation atColumbia University in New York; the Institute for Advanced Studies in Science Technology and Society at Graz University of Technology; the Agora Energiewende in Berlin and the Max Planck Institute for the Study of Societies in Cologne. She has led several research projects on climate and energy politics and on new energy technologies funded by the National Science Centre, the European Commission and the Polish-German Science Foundation.

Routledge Focus on Environment and Sustainability

For more information about this series, please visit: https://www.routledge.com/Routledge-Focus-on-Environment-and-Sustainability/book-series/RFES

Climate and Energy Politics in Poland

Debating Carbon Dioxide and Shale Gas

Aleksandra Lis

Routledge
Taylor & Francis Group
LONDON AND NEW YORK

earthscan
from Routledge

First published 2020 by Routledge

2 Park Square, Milton Park, Abingdon, Oxon OX14 4RN
605 Third Avenue, New York, NY 10017

Routledge is an imprint of the Taylor & Francis Group, an informa business

First issued in paperback 2021

Publisher's Note

The publisher has gone to great lengths to ensure the quality of this reprint
but points out that some imperfections in the original copies may be apparent.

British Library Cataloguing-in-Publication Data
A catalogue record for this book is available from the British Library

Library of Congress Cataloging-in-Publication Data
A catalog record has been requested for this book

ISBN: 978-0-367-19549-6 (hbk)
ISBN: 978-1-03-217296-5 (pbk)
DOI: 10.4324/9780429203091

Typeset in Times New Roman
by Newgen Publishing UK

To my family and friends

Contents

Acknowledgements

I would like to thank the Ministry of Science and Higher Education in Poland for providing me with the perfect conditions for writing this book within the fellowship programme "Mobilność Plus" (1616/MOB/V/2017/0), as part of which I spent nine months at the Center for Science, Technology, Medicine & Society at the University of California, Berkeley. This would not have been possible without the kind invitation from the Director of the Center, Professor Massimo Mazzotti. I would also like to thank the National Science Centre of Poland for granting me with funding for collecting data on shale gas within a research project titled "Shale gas as a new challenge for Europe: re-thinking the role of expertise in European integration processes" (2013/11/D/HS6/04715).

I would also like to extend my gratitude to the many colleagues who engaged in conversations with me about the book project and commented on the proposal and the manuscript, especially Randi Heinrichs, Rafał Szymanowski, Daniel Kim, Mario Sacomano Neto, Zofia Boni and Łukasz Afeltowicz. I am also grateful for the continuous support from my colleagues at the Institute of Ethnology and Cultural Anthropology at Adam Mickiewicz University in Poznań, especially Izabella Main, Kacper Pobłocki and Michał Buchowski. I also extend my thanks to my supervisors at the Central European University in Budapest, Alexandra Kowalski and Balazs Vedres, who helped me to write my dissertation on "Making a Market: The Problem of Polish Carbon in EU Climate Politics", which constitutes a substantial basis for large parts of this book. Special thanks also go to Agata Stasik for an enjoyable cooperation on shale gas development in local communities within the project "Shale gas as a new challenge for Europe: re-thinking the role of expertise in European integration processes" (2013/11/D/HS6/04715).

This book would not have been possible without the openness and patience of so many of my interviewees, who spent many hours with me discussing the different and intricate issues of Poland's energy politics, the politics of constructing the European carbon market and shale gas development. In particular, I would like to show my appreciation to the experts from the Polish Geological Institute, who explained to me the technicalities of their valuable work so that I could fully understand the impacts of shale gas extraction on the natural environment, and to the trade union leaders and experts who helped me to understand how the reduction of carbon dioxide emissions will impact the Polish economy and the futures of employees in many different sectors. Special thanks also go to the many other experts, officials, MEPs and activists at various institutions in Poland and Brussels.

Last but not least, I would like to thank my dear family and friends who believed in my work, cheered me on and provided me with many welcome distractions.

Abbreviations

CBOS	Centre for Public Opinion Research
CEE	Central and Eastern Europe
DGEP	Directorate-General for Environmental Protection
EDF	Environmental Defense Fund
EIA	Energy Information Agency
EIT	Economy in Transition
EMCEF	European Mine, Chemical and Energy Workers Federation
EMF	European Metalworkers' Federation
ETUC	European Trade Union Confederation
EUA	European Union Allowance
EU ETS	European Union Emissions Trading System
FZZ	Trade Unions' Forum
ICFTU	International Confederation of Free Trade Unions
IFIEC Europe	International Federation of Industrial Energy Consumers (Europe)
IG BCE	IG Bergbau, Chemie, Energie
IPCC	Intergovernmental Panel for Climate Change
IPPC	Integrated Pollution and Prevention Control
JRC	Joint Research Centre
NAP	National Allocation Plan
NCBiR	National Centre for Research and Development
NEPP	National Environmental Policy Plan
NGO	non-governmental organization
NOKE	National Operator of Energy Minerals
NSZZ Solidarność	Independent Self-Governing Trade Union Solidarność
OPZZ	All-Poland Alliance of Trade Unions

PGI	Polish Geological Institute
TPPs	tradable pollution permits
TUAC	Trade Union Advisory Committee
TUSDAC	Trade Unions for Sustainable Development Advisory Committee
UH Network	European Science and Technology Network on UKIE Office of the European Integration Committee
	Unconventional Hydrocarbon Extraction
UNFCCC	United Nations Framework Convention on Climate Change
USGS	US Geological Survey
VIK	Verband der Industriellen Energie- und Kraftwirtschaft
WWF	World Wide Fund for Nature

Introduction

I was standing in the middle of a vast corn field in Champaign, Illinois, looking at a set of curved pipes and valves sticking out from the ground – an underground injection point for industrial carbon dioxide. It was extremely hot and the sun was blinding us, as the protective glasses that we had been given by the hosts were not tinted. The area belonged to an ethanol producer, and we could see some industrial buildings in the distance. I stood on ground in which carbon dioxide was stored deep below my feet. At the time of our visit no underground injection was taking place, but normally carbon dioxide would enter the ground through these curved pipes, transported through a long pipeline leading from the ethanol-producing facility. The underground storage was a few thousand metres deep. The project being carried out by the ethanol company, in cooperation with scientists from the National Sequestration Education Center, was a pilot project, but industrial-scale carbon capture and storage technology is one of the climate change mitigation solutions recommended by the Intergovernmental Panel for Climate Change (IPCC). However, as the risks of storing carbon dioxide underground are not yet known, projects such the one in Illinois are being used to study how carbon dioxide behaves underground. It was an exciting visit, as for the first time in my life I could almost sense the materiality of the carbon dioxide emitted by industries, something that is usually quite abstract and that we only read about in reports and newspapers. I hadn't yet sensed it, but I could see the pipes through which it was transported and I could feel the ground below my feet in which it was being stored.

Carbon dioxide has its own material properties. For example, it dissolves well in saline water but it is not easily sequestrated from industrial or power sector emissions. It is also difficult to transform it into something economically useful. As a greenhouse gas causing climate change, it needs to be reduced from the atmosphere, and one way to achieve this is to simply pump it underground and store it there forever. This book examines carbon dioxide as a material object enmeshed in various economic and social contexts of electricity and industrial production, both of which are crucial for contemporary economic systems.

Energy production is responsible for 35 percent of global anthropogenic greenhouse gas emission, yet it can also be thought of as a blood circulation system for today's economies. It is important for economic growth, for citizens to carry on with their daily lives, and for states to secure their geopolitical interests. However, faced with the present climate crisis, we are no longer able to divorce energy production and consumption from its impact on the climate. This conclusion, repeated time and again at successive climate change summits, has finally resulted in the establishment of a new policy nexus, which has been termed in policy studies as "a climate change and energy security nexus" (Kuzemko 2013). However, the shift from thinking about energy in relation to economic growth or state security alone to putting it into the context of the changing climate has not been achieved everywhere, and this book presents the reader with some examples of difficulties regarding this shift faced by the largest member state of the European Union (EU) from Central and Eastern Europe (CEE) – Poland – a country with a long legacy of coal extraction and a dependency on burning coal for electricity production. What additionally complicates attempts to construct an energy security–climate change nexus in Poland is the fact that Polish industries and households still in 2014, relied on Russian gas and oil supplies for around 70 percent of demand for gas and about 93 percent for oil (Kublik 2014). Today this dependency is lower. This geopolitical factor makes it difficult for Polish state actors to favour (Russian) gas over (largely domestic) coal. Therefore, after Poland's accession to the EU in 2004, two issues became central to the economic and political concerns of consequent Polish governments: diversification of natural gas supplies and the reduction of carbon dioxide emissions.

While the economic transition of the 1990s was carried out with a sense of entitlement to quick economic growth, according to the adopted imagery of "finally catching up with the West" (Buchowski 2006; Dunn 2004), the EU's climate change policies ultimately complicated this conviction. Who had the right to economic growth in times of climate change, in today's climate crisis? The answers given by the Polish elites revealed a sense of irresponsibility with regard to global environmental challenges. From the 1990s to the present day, politicians and business actors alike have been accustomed to demanding solidarity from other countries on their own path to development. Solidarity with countries touched by climate change has commonly been perceived in Poland as not being "our duty". During the Kyoto negotiations, CEE countries, including Poland, were listed as economies in transition (EIT), which gave them leeway on emission reduction. However, as the EU began to pursue its own climate change goals, relying on the European Union Emissions Trading System (EU ETS) as its main policy tool, it gradually broke away from a 'special treatment' strategy for CEE countries. From 2013 onwards, CEE economic actors had to abide by the same rules as Western EU member states and commit to radical reductions in carbon dioxide emissions. This demanded a new kind of energy politics, new strategies, tools and goals, new concepts, new language and new ways of thinking about the role of the Polish economy both in the EU and globally.

The shift towards climate policies in the EU coincided with a shale gas boom in the USA and a growing interest in the extraction of this resource in Europe. Poland jumped on this project with great enthusiasm and set out to build new relations with global oil and gas companies, foreign national geological surveys and various experts in this area. This, I argue, complicated the existing energy politics of the Polish state even further. It has also complicated what I refer to as the scalar politics of the Polish state, by which I mean the relations of the Polish state and economic actors with other actors in Europe and beyond. Climate mitigation policies and shale gas development alike have, at times, made it cumbersome for the Polish actors to identify with the EU's goals, and difficult to accommodate Polish interests in EU policies. The issues around carbon dioxide emissions and shale gas have also challenged the existing relations between the Polish state and its citizens, as various citizen groups began to take an active stance in debates on the environmental and social impacts of various industrial activities and to educate themselves in what energy transition may look like in Poland. Therefore, I argue, similarly to other energy sources (such as coal and oil) which have in the past re-scaled state politics and changed relations between actors in regional and global economic systems (Mitchell 2011); carbon dioxide and shale gas have come to interfere with the social, political and economic orders in post-accession Poland. Each has played an important role in shaping energopolitics (Boyer 2011), challenging the productive powers of the Polish state, and shifting configurations of actors within which power over energy and through energy could be exercised.

This book addresses one specific aspect of the challenges outlined above, that of expertise production about carbon dioxide and shale gas, which entered the political scene in Poland and complicated the existing notions of energy politics. This, in turn, forced actors to forge new relations – both conceptual and material – to go beyond business and politics "as usual". Conceptually, I seek to grasp these processes through the idiom of co-production (Jasanoff 2004), which makes it possible to examine how expertise and sociopolitical orders co-emerge and how they shape each other in a mutual way. This mutual influence has a material dimension that I also account for in this book, which positions it within various types of social science literature, such as the material semiotic tradition (Law 2007) of the social studies of science, technology and society (STS), with its recent interest in carbon trade (Callon 2009; MacKenzie 2007a, 2007b, 2008); anthropology, with its long-lasting tradition of studying how material objects help humans to organize societies; and political ecology, which together with human geography proposes conceptualizations of resources as outcomes of political economic processes (Escobar 1995; see Kama 2019 for an example that includes shale gas).

The implications of climate policies and shale gas development, which can be recognized locally, regionally and globally, made it difficult to decide what scale is relevant for the required expertise. Should Polish actors speak only about impacts on the national economy? What makes up the national economy in an economically interlinked world? And what about environmental impacts? How do we speak about Polish interests if the future of the Earth is at risk? Are national or sectorial solidarities still of relevance for global climate action? How do we draw the lines of European solidarities? All these questions make the co-production perspective even more relevant, especially once we realize that expertise is also involved in scaling social orders into different scales of governance. More specifically, I am talking here about a mutually constitutive relation between expertise on carbon dioxide and shale gas, and state and EU institutions. "States, we may say, are made of knowledge, just as knowledge is constituted by states" (Jasanoff 2004, p. 3). In this sense, the book engages with the relation between knowledge production about carbon dioxide and shale gas by various actors and the re-construction of the Polish state and EU as scalar structures of governance.

The account given in the book shows how Polish state actors and those involved in the country's energy sector found it difficult to define what the climate–energy security nexus could mean for the state and its economy. Two debates that illustrate very well the gravity of this challenge are: (1) the debate on the 2020 Climate Change and Energy Package in 2008–2009 and (2) the debate about shale gas extraction in EU countries in 2011–2016. While the first debate was a wake-up call for Poland to realize that it had become part of ambitious EU climate change policies, in the second debate Polish actors tried to actively re-define shale gas as a viable energy option in the EU. Whereas in the first debate, Polish actors mobilized their resources to produce expertise and political justifications to obtain an exemption from EU climate and energy regulations, in the second debate they acted strategically to block any additional EU-level environmental regulations that could limit shale gas extraction or make it more costly. The cases that I study in this book can thus also be understood as examples of how energopolitics came to shape wider socio-economic and political orders. This involves three processes: (1) the making of two energy objects, carbon dioxide and shale gas; (2) the construction of a climate–energy security nexus through political discourse and expert knowledge production; and (3) the re-scaling of knowledge production about economic, political and environmental impacts and structures of governance and publics. These three processes are interconnected and the two objects (carbon dioxide and shale gas) are not passively involved in knowledge pro-duction and politics, but rather their materiality puts limits on these processes.

The book covers around ten years of the post-accession history of Poland with regard to climate and energy politics and is based on ori-ginal research which, to a large extent, has not been published thus far. I collected the data analysed in this book over the course of the past ten years, as part of five different research projects. Around two hundred interviews were conducted with CEE actors, mainly in Poland and in Brussels. On over thirty occasions, I took part as an observer at climate, energy and shale gas-related events in Poland and Europe. Additionally, a systematic media analysis and policy document analysis were carried out. Thus, the book offers new insights through the interpretation of systematically collected data.

Energy objects and co-production of scales

The idea that some parts of the natural environment can be distinguished as objects of human activity relies on an ontological distinction that we are used to making between nature and society (Latour 1999). In the 1970s, through the environmental sciences, this Cartesian dualism was transformed into a "Nature plus Society arithmetic" (Moore 2015). For example, earth-system scientists talk about "coupled human–natural systems"; Marxist ecologists speak of the "nature–society dialectic"; and cultural studies highlight hybrids, assemblages and networks (Moore 2015, p. 33–34). Moore poses a similar question to the ones asked by Latour (1999) and Haraway (2015) about the possibilities of thinking, speaking and acting in a non-dualistic way. He criticizes our perception of nature as something exogenous to human history, as a tap of resources and a sink of pollution (Moore 2015, p. 33). Similarly to Latour (1999), Moore seeks vocabularies and analytical lenses for translating "the materialist, dialectical, and holistic philosophy of humans-*in*-nature" (p. 33). This would seem to be a Latourian point made from a perspective of the problem of resource extraction, stemming from a need to understand modern capitalism. Humans-*in*-nature should be seen as humans in a matrix rather than humans plus nature: "Nature, instead, becomes the matrix within which human activity unfolds, and the field upon which historical agency operates" (Moore 2015, p. 36). From this perspective, says Moore (2015), the problems of food, water, oil, and also carbon dioxide and gas, "become relational problems first and object problems second; through the relations of specific civilizations, food, water, and oil become real historical actors" (p. 36). Similarly, the problem of agency is not to be seen solely as a property of either humans or nature but as "an emergent property of definite configurations of human activity with the rest of life" (Moore 2015, p 36). This type of relationality and objectification constitutes an important perspective for this book, which examines how carbon dioxide and shale gas are entangled in this matrix, in the web of life, economic and political systems. State power in the field of energy policies, to follow Moore (2015), can thus be seen as deriving from and unfolding through specific configurations and (re-)productions in the web of life (Moore 2015, p. 37).

According to Moore (2015), in contemporary economic systems configurations of state agency cannot be examined without embedding them in nature-in-capitalism relations. The accumulation of capital cannot be seen outside of nature or simply as a result of interacting with nature, but rather as a bundling of human and extra-human natures (Moore 2015, p. 43). In this sense, the conditions, including the limits, of both nature and capitalism are co-produced in the interwoven matrix between the two. Adding expertise to this co-productionist configuration of nature as matrix and economic systems helps us to understand how the field of nature is changing, and how capital is not only able to grasp, approach and internalize this change, but also creates conditions for expertise to be produced. At the same time, despite the usefulness of this perspective, we cannot escape actors' own conceptualizations of the web of life, which are usually formed through an objectifying lens. Objectification makes it possible to act upon the web of life, even at the cost of obscuring the actual character of this relation. Therefore, in this book both perspectives are present: the objectifying view, discourses and practices of actors involved in reducing carbon dioxide and developing shale gas, and a "nature as matrix" perspective through which I try to critically understand the unfolding reality.

This analytical move of dismantling the boundaries between nature as a resource and sociopolitical systems is not new. Almost a decade ago, Timothy Mitchell suggested not thinking separately about democracy and oil, but rather about "democracy *as* oil" (Mitchell 2011, p. 5). When transposed to the recent case of Poland, this claim can be rephrased as the "Polish sociopolitical system as coal", and the emergence of carbon dioxide and shale gas has resulted in tension between the prospect of their smooth integration into that system or of that system's transformation. This perspective seems particularly valid when we observe that thinking about energy politics through carbon dioxide and shale gas has to be re-scaled from a dominant binary relation, domestic vs. foreign (Russian), to the more complex EU and global relations. The fear of Russia (Zarzycki 2004) is deeply rooted in political discourse in Poland, and the fear of Russian gas, of a dependency on the Russian resources, comprises an important part of it. Carbon dioxide, and in particular shale gas, have provided yet another opportunity for Poland to detach itself from the East – the de-Orientalization of Poland as an economic and political space – and to escape the influence of Russia. Within a binary scale of East and West, "domestic coal" meant state security and "Russian gas" a potential threat (Szulecki 2018). However, climate changed introduce a new scale – of low-carbon and carbon-intensive fossil fuels – with coal being the more dangerous and natural gas being the less dangerous fuel for the climate. Therefore, climate policies forced Polish political and business elites had to re-think the status of "domestic coal as a national treasure" and Poland's "black gold" (see Kuchler and Bridge 2018), as they gradually realized how much they would have to pay for burning this "treasure".

Shale gas has complicated this picture even more. With the assessment of potential shale gas resources in Poland by the US Energy Information Agency (EIA 2011), there emerged some completely new possibilities for economic development. The established narrative was not only about the possibility of cutting down on Russian gas imports but on gas imports in general. Moreover, for the first time in history, Poland could become an exporter of natural gas – "the second Kuwait or Norway" (see Lis and Stankiewicz 2017). The scalar politics of shale gas changed relations with Poland's Eastern neighbour, Russia. Soon, however, it became clear that the politics of shale gas extraction were not solely about the economics of a new energy resource. The experience with hydraulic fracturing ("fracking"), mainly in the United States, triggered concerns about the environmental impacts of shale gas and oil extraction. Through social media, these concerns quickly exceeded the local scales of communities' experience and concerns. An anti-fracking movement made up of community members and activists from non-governmental organizations (NGOs) was established to find political support in European countries, including France and Germany, and in EU institutions and the European Parliament. This movement also involved local Polish communities, first by weaving links between French/Brussels activists and local communities in the Pomeranian region, and then between activists in the UK and United States and activists in Poland's Lubelskie region (Lis and Stasik 2017). And although impacts on climate change have not always figured at the forefront of the activists' banners, a wave of opposition against fracking was motivated by pro-climate objectives to eradicate all fossil fuels from energy production and replace them with renewable energy sources. This once again complicated the scalar politics that the Polish state got involved in through the shale gas development project. The shift from dependence on Russian gas towards independence and export was challenging enough; having to face the European Parliament, the European Commission and the global anti-fracking opposition was another matter.

EU accession and the de-Orientalization of expertise

The focus of this book on knowledge production is justified by an argument that EU accession changed the position of Poland within the global system of knowledge production. Prior to EU accession, during the Kyoto Protocol negotiations in the 1990s, Poland and other CEE countries were listed under the Annex I Parties as economies in transition (EIT). In this way a special category of countries was created with assigned emission reduction targets tailored to their economic situation. Poland could argue for "the right to development", "the right to catch up with the developed world", and make claims for having a lower responsibility for climate change. The EU as a regional organization was listed under Annex I. The argument that I make in this book says that, with EU accession, CEE countries gained a dual status as an EIT and as an Annex I Party through EU membership. With this shift, when it came to devising policy instruments for complying with the Kyoto targets, as the EU was obliged to do, all economic differences between the CEE member states and the original member states had to be dealt with within the EU. Debates about these differences intensified in the context of climate and energy policies when the European Commission proposed the same rules for all energy producers participating within the European Union Emissions Trading System (EU ETS). The EU ETS has been the EU's main policy instrument for meeting its Kyoto and other emissions reduction targets.

I argue in this book that this shift in classification through EU accession, from a developing to a developed economy, resulted in a de-Orientalization (see Escobar 1995) of the whole CEE region as an object of knowledge production. I propose speaking of de-Orientalization as a disenchantment of the CEE region, including Poland. I argue that while de-Orientalization started with the transition processes of the 1980s/ 1990s (Buchowski 2006), EU accession was a breakthrough moment for the region, as it shifted the attention of the Western, developed and liberal parts of the world away from it. Buchowski (2017) refers de-Orientalizing distinctions to individual actors in post-transition Poland and the relations between them. I refer de-Orientalizing policies and political discourses to the Polish economy as a space of governance in post-accession Poland. The argument that I make in this book is that, prior to EU accession, the CEE region was seen as a space of disorder, a space that needed to be described, disciplined and re-organized. After EU accession, once EU institutions became the main disciplining actors for CEE, the region started to be perceived as part of the ordered, Western world. EU institutions became the main actors producing knowledge about CEE, usually in an aggregate way. Differences between the EU's East and West had to be negotiated internally, within the EU club of member states. In other words, having joined the EU, CEE countries changed their position from being part of the developing world (if not Orientalized as the Third World then at least as the Second World) to being part of the developed world. I argue that with EU accession, CEE countries lost their significance in terms of the "development discourse" (Escobar 1995).

However this shift apparently did not help Poland to strengthen its own capacity to produce knowledge about its economic system. Weak and relatively poor expert institutions made it difficult for Poland to quickly assess the impacts of EU legislation or to propose new solutions for itself (for an example featuring analysis about a different area of policy, the eurozone crisis, see Matthijs 2016). There are only three or four think tanks that analyse problems related to electricity markets and regulations in the power sector, and there are none that are dedicated to energy transition – one of the main projects of the EU today. Thus, it has quickly become clear that in post-accession Poland, expertise production still depended on access to resources coming from outside the country, and that tapping into these resources demanded the establishment of extensive networks of relations, going far beyond the borders of the nation state. In the context of EU accession, this was a new skill to be mastered – the skill of playing scalar politics, of navigating networks of relations without losing sight of one's goals. These struggles for self-definition in political and policy terms will be examined in this book in the context of climate, energy and resource politics.

Indeed, when the European Commission proposed its Climate Change and Energy Package in January 2008, the Polish government did not even realize its potentially negative impacts on the Polish economy. And since the Commission's Impact Assessment study accompanying the package of directives calculated the impacts of the proposed reform on "an average EU economy", the exceptionally difficult situation of the Polish economy under the reformed EU ETS was not made clear. The gravity of the situation stemmed from the fact that Polish power plants would have to pay around 40 euros for each tonne of carbon dioxide emitted – and with around 90 percent of electricity produced from coal, there would be many tonnes of carbon dioxide to pay for. Neither the Polish government nor the power sector were able to quickly assess in numbers the potential impact on the Polish economy. Shale gas extraction brought about yet another shift in knowledge production processes in Poland. The first impulse for a growing interest in unconventional hydrocarbon resources in Poland came from the United States, specifically the US Energy Information Agency in 2011. The capital attracted by the Polish state administration for investment in exploration activities was global, coming mainly from Western European and Northern American countries. The Polish government and Polish geological services established diplomatic relations with the US Geological Survey, as well as with the Chinese authorities. As will be revealed, it took quite long time and an unusually large mobilization of people and resources to fully understand the Polish situation within these new schemes.

The emphasis placed on knowledge production leads us to reflect on the role of experts. Rose and Miller (1992) point to the role of knowledge in modern government, understood not simply as "ideas" but as "the vast assemblage of persons, theories, projects, experiments and techniques that has become such a central component of government" (p. 177). The government has become a problematizing activity with a "claim to certain knowledge of the sphere or problem to be addressed" (Rose and Miller 1992, p. 182). Knowledge itself becomes subjected to various rules of selection and legitimation. For example, in one of the cases examined in this book, expertise on the EU ETS becomes qualified as "the Commission's proposal", "the IFIEC's proposal", "the Polish government's proposal", inscribed into particular configurations of actors, and thus cannot be seen as neutral.

Expertise has the potential to span different fields of action and connect various actors, as it is usually devised in such a way as to scale problems and solutions in a textual way and through networks of actors who find them relevant. Having said that, in this book I study not only how mitigating carbon dioxide emissions and developing shale gas extraction opportunities were framed by Polish actors, but also how these actors wove relations with other, foreign actors to make their framing and expertise, relevant on two different scales: national and European. This also helps us to understand why there is no universal boundary between politics, economics and expert institutions, but these are constantly being organized and re-defined in discourses and shifting relations. When conceptualizing the type of work carried out by experts, Eyal and Buchholtz (2010) refer to Latour's theorization of the work of scientists. According to Latour (1987), scientists neither "discover objective facts" nor "socially construct" them. They "'recruit", "mobilize" and forge alliances with the objects they study, and there is a certain materiality to this process. Experts, by producing expertise, inscribe relations between actors and issues into various material devices, mainly into different forms of written textual reports, policy briefs and position papers. At the same time, Eyal and Pok (2011) point out that one should differentiate between experts and expertise, as the latter is not a mere attribute of the former. Expertise is "a network connecting together actors, instruments, statements and institutional arrangements" (p. 1). Different local realities are being connected and translated within those networks of expertise.

Looking at the EU as a governance structure, expert knowledge has become an immanent part of European governance (Nowotny 2003; Boswell 2008; Egeberg et al. 2003). This can be seen in various policy areas. The EU's decision to take the lead in global climate action and the interlinking of environmental and energy problems make various types of expert knowledge even more necessary. At the same time, what is being discussed is the allocation of these problems and policy solutions to the "right" level of governance – at the European, national and sometimes even local level. Through the controversial technology of hydraulic fracturing, shale gas exploration has come to represent a perfect case of ambiguous scaling, as it raises concerns about energy security, environmental protection, and the distribution of risks and benefits, all of which require negotiations at the correct scale.

Thus, this book studies various interventions of expertise (Eyal and Buchholtz 2010) as interventions into European and Polish scalar politics. By scalar politics I mean attempts to define the EU, its member states and local communities as distinct levels that appear to publics as separate, fairly bounded spaces of governance. In other words, the European, national and local levels of shale gas governance will be studied not as given and objective spaces, but rather as spaces that are produced through actors' interactions, in the course of which they may be contested and questioned (Simons et al. 2014). One of the goals of the book is to provide answers to fundamental questions about how expertise is produced and how we can define this process in a sociologically meaningful way. This seems particularly vital in an era where citizens are increasing their participation in technological controversies affecting the EU (Brossard 2008; Kurath and Gisler 2009). How are the new publics around environmental and technological issues mobilized and constituted and how do they produce legitimate knowledge? How are citizens and their knowledge and sensibilities mobilized into policy-making processes (Valerie Burri 2009; Wynne 1991)? And how does environmental knowledge produce new subjectivities?

Roadmap of the book

Chapter 1 – New energy objects and the (de-)Orientalization of Poland

This chapter outlines how carbon dioxide and, later on, shale gas became objects of energy politics in the context of post-socialist transformation and EU membership. Each case is discussed separately, but the common goal is to show how the making of these two objects involved various non-domestic actors and how in each case the process was inscribed into the various political and economic agendas of these actors. In this chapter, I am interested in understanding how the making of these two objects formed part of the Orientalizing and de-Orientalizing discourses about Poland during recent decades. In both stories, US-based actors were the first to introduce new objects – carbon dioxide and shale gas – to the political agendas of the ruling Polish government. However, in both cases, it was the EU that stabilized its existence in relation to energy and climate politics and established itself as a reference point for the further discourses and actions of Polish actors.

Chapter 2 – Production of expertise, scaling and carbon dioxide in Poland

As the story of this chapter unfolds, it becomes apparent that while fighting for their interests in the EU, Polish actors had to reflect on their own position in relation to other actors. The first reaction from Poland to the proposal of the new EU ETS by the European Commission was to ask for an opt-out from the full actions of the EU Allowances for its electricity producers. This story is analysed from two angles. First, it is shown that several political scalar effects (Simons et al. 2014) of various spaces of governance are co-produced (Jasanoff 2004) through different processes of expertise production and the negotiation of it: the nation state, the CEE region, Eastern and Western Europe, and the EU as an integrated space of governance. Moreover, a new object is co-produced, which turns out to be politically and economically scalable – carbon dioxide emissions. Depending on the policy proposal, carbon dioxide has been objectified in relation to different actors (power companies), spaces (various regions of Europe), fossil fuels (coal and gas) and geo-politics (Russia or Western Europe). It is objectified as an object with a socialist legacy, as an object of traumatic post-socialist transition and as an object involved in modernization and economic development, and each objectification is conducive to a different scale of political action, to different politics.

Chapter 3 – Production of expertise, scaling and shale gas in Poland

In this chapter, I argue that shale gas in Poland constitutes a particularly important energy object, valued mainly as a strategic resource for the economy and Poland's energy security. In 2011, the US Energy Information Agency (EIA 2011) published an assessment of natural gas and oil resources in shale rock formations worldwide. According to the report, Poland had the second largest reserve of unconventional natural gas resources of all European countries, second only to France. With these numbers shale gas entered energy politics in Poland as a potential highly valuable resource. However, given its materiality – shale gas being trapped over three thousand metres below the surface – significant capital and expertise needed to be invested in order to transform it into a resource, which in the end failed. Moreover, through EU membership, shale gas is contextualized by the energy security–climate change nexus and other environmental concerns. EU institutions played an important role in bringing these extra-economic and extra-security valuations of shale gas to the forefront. The short history of shale gas exploration in Poland – a couple of years of debates and subsoil activities – places Poland in the new context of resource politics. In this chapter, I argue that an interesting dependency is created: all knowledge-producing actors depend on capital investment in resource exploration. Without this involvement, there is no data to operate on, to make plans or predictions about the economic and environmental future of the project. In other words, global capital is an important part of co-production of the different kinds of expertise about the resource and the resource itself.

Chapter 4 – Co-production of sociopolitical orders: energy objects, publics and states

This chapter describes the processes through which objectification of carbon dioxide and shale gas co-produces broader sociopolitical orders in terms of the relations between states and publics. The first part of the chapter focuses on the co-production of new categories of workers along a scale of "cleanness", on which different jobs may be positioned as "clean/green" or "dirty/black" depending on the amount of carbon dioxide emitted based on the work performed by humans and machines together. The existing human and machine constellations at different production sites began to account for a new actor – carbon dioxide. The existence or non-existence of this object, as well as its intensity in production processes, starts to matter when jobs are compared, valued, saved or abandoned. Carbon dioxide as a greenhouse gas introduces a new political dimension to the discussion about jobs in Europe. In this chapter, I examine how trade union representatives from Poland negotiated their own presence on a new scale of clean and dirty jobs.

In the second part of the chapter, I analyse how shale gas politics co-produce different publics at different scales, local, regional, national and European, and how within these publics various relations between states and citizens are negotiated. Shale gas as an object was not only constructed and co-produced by experts, administrations and companies; it was also objectified (and sometimes objected to) by local communities in various parts of Poland. Being strongly politicized by the Polish government, shale gas entered public debate in the media and in local conversations in many communities loaded with hopes and fears. As the shale gas development project unfolded in various operations carried out by companies, yet another object became politicized among local inhabitants: post-fracking waste. Its visibility and invisibility, and its association and disassociation with shale gas exploration in Poland, shaped relations of trust and mistrust between Polish citizens and state institutions.

Conclusion: CEE countries and the challenge of knowledge production

The conclusion chapter provides a reflection on the challenges of knowledge production in the CEE region in the new context of the energy security–climate nexus and EU accession. First, it is important to consider whether CEE actors have the capacity to produce knowledge about themselves and how this can be made politically efficient for their own interests. These questions involve reflecting on the processes of re-scaling CEE states, which struggle to find a relevant scale for their own politics around climate and energy issues. However, it is also important to consider whether, in an interconnected world, when faced with the global challenge of climate change and with low knowledge production capacities, they are capable of defining the scale of their action on their own. Second, the place and role of development discourse in the CEE region needs re-thinking. One vital question is whether development discourse can still work for this region. What kinds of actors – Western or CEE – are interested in practising this discourse? And if only CEE actors are interested in maintaining a development discourse about themselves, then does discourse still "do the same things" for the CEE region as it did when it was practised by Western actors?

References

Boswell, C. (2008) The political functions of expert knowledge: knowledge and legitimation in European Union immigration policy. *Journal of European Public Policy* 15(4): 471–488.

Boyer, D. (2011) Energopolitics and the anthropology of energy. *Anthropology News* 52: 5–7.

Brossard, D. (2008) Media, scientific journals and science communication: examining the construction of scientific controversies. *Public Understanding of Science* 18(3): 258–274.

Buchowski, M. (2006) The specter of Orientalism in Europe: from exotic Other to stigmatized brother. *Anthropological Quarterly* 79(3): 463–482.

Buchowski, M. (2017) *Czyściec: Antropologia neoliberalnego postsocjalizmu.* Wydawnictwo Naukowe UAM.

Burri, V. R. (2009) Coping with uncertainty: assessing nanotechnologies in a citizen panel in Switzerland. *Public Understanding of Science* 18(5): 498–511.

Callon, M. (2009) Civilizing markets: carbon trading between in vitro and in vivo experiments. *Accounting, Organizations and Society* 34(3/4): 535–548.

Dunn, E. (2004) *Privatizing Poland: Baby Food, Big Business, and the Remaking of Labor.* Ithaca, NY: Cornell University Press.

Egeberg, M., Schaefer, G. and Trondal, J. (2003) The many faces of EU committee governance. *West European Politics* 26(3): 19–40.

Energy Information Administration (EIA). (2011) *World Shale Gas Resources: An Initial Assessment of 14 Regions Outside I United States.* Retrieved 14 January 2014 from www.eia.gov/analysis/studies/worldshalegas/archive/2011/pdf/fullreport.pdf

Escobar, A. (1995) *Encountering Development: The Making and Unmaking of the Third World*. Princeton, NJ: Princeton University Press.

Eyal, G. and Buchholtz, L. (2010) From the sociology of intellectuals to the sociology of interventions. *Annual Review of Sociology* 36: 117–137.

Eyal, G. and Pok, G. (2011) From a sociology of professions to a sociology of expertise. Retrieved 27 October 2019 from www.semanticscholar.org/paper/ From-a-sociology-of-professions-to-a-sociology-of-Eyal-Pok/e0fba82e8e40 aba82e8ea0e771b3d228d0ce30c4

Haraway, D. (2015) Anthropocene, capitalocene, plantationocene, chthulucene: making kin. *Environmental Humanities* 6(1): 159–165.

Jasanoff, S. (ed.) (2004) *States of Knowledge: The Co-Production of Science and Social Order*. London: Routledge.

Kama, K. (2019) Resource-making controversies: knowledge, anticipatory politics and economization of unconventional fossil fuels. *Progress in Human Geography*. https://doi.org/10.1177/0309132519829223

Kuchler, M. and Bridge, G. (2018) Down the black hole: sustaining national socio-technical imaginaries of coal in Poland. *Energy Research & Social Science* 41: 136–147.

Kurath, M., and Gisler, P. (2009) Informing, involving or engaging? Science communication, in the ages of atom-, bio- and nanotechnology. *Public Understanding of Science* 18(5): 559–573.

Kuzemko, C. (2013) *The Energy Security–Climate Nexus: Institutional Change in the UK and Beyond*. London: Palgrave Macmillan.

Latour, B. (1987) *Science in Action: How to Follow Scientists and Engineers through Society*. Cambridge, MA: Harvard University Press.

Latour, B. (1999) *The Politics of Nature: How to Bring the Sciences into Democracy*. Cambridge, MA: Harvard University Press.

Law, J. (2007) *Actor Network Theory and Material Semiotics*. Version of 25 April 2007. Retrieved 18 May 2007 from www.heterogeneities.net/publications/ Law2007ANTandMaterialSemiotics.pdf

Lis, A. and Stankiewicz, P. (2017) Framing shale gas for policy-making in Poland. *Journal of Environmental Policy and Planning* 19(1): 53–71.

Lis, A. and Stasik, A. (2017) Hybrid forums, knowledge deficits and the multiple uncertainties of resource extraction: negotiating the local governance of shale gas in Poland. *Energy Research & Social Science* 28: 29–36.

MacKenzie, D. (2007a) Finding the ratchet: the political economy of carbon trading. Unpublished essay. Retrieved 26 January 2020 from www.sociology. ed.ac.uk/__data/assets/pdf_file/0015/3417/DMacKenzieRatchet16.pdf

MacKenzie, D. (2007b) The political economy of carbon trading. *London Review of Books* 29: 29–31.

MacKenzie, D. (2008) Making things the same: gases, emission rights and the politics of carbon markets. *Accounting, Organizations and Society* 34(3–4): 440–455.

Matthijs, M. (2016) The euro's "winner-take-all" political economy: institutional choices, policy drift, and divergent patterns of inequality. *Politics & Society* 44(3): 393–422.

Mitchell, T. (2011) *Carbon Democracy: Political Power in the Age of Oil.* London: Verso.

Moore, J. W. (2015) *Capitalism in the Web of Life: Ecology and the Accumulation of Capital.* London: Verso.

Nowotny, H. (2003) Democratising expertise and socially robust knowledge. *Science and Public Policy* 30(3): 151–156.

Rose, N. and Miller, P. (1992) Political power beyond the state: problematics of government. *The British Journal of Sociology* 43(2): 173–205.

Simons, A., Lis, A. and Lippert, I. (2014) The political duality of scale-making in environmental markets. *Environmental Politics* 23(4): 632–649.

Szulecki, K. (ed.) (2018) *Energy Security in Europe: Divergent Perceptions and Policy Challenges.* Cham: Palgrave Macmillan.

Wynne, B. (1991) Knowledges in context. *Science, Technology & Human Values* 16(1): 111–121.

Zarycki, T. (2004) Uses of Russia: the role of Russia in the modern Polish national identity. *East European Politics & Societies* 18(4): 595–627.

Media report

Kublik, A. (2014) Europa i Polska mocno uzależnione od gazu i ropy z Rosji. *Gazeta Wyborcza* (24 March 2014). Retrieved from http://wyborcza.pl/1,155287,15673381,Europa_i_Polska_mocno_uzaleznione_od_gazu_i_ropy_z.html

1 New energy objects and the (de-)Orientalization of Poland

Introduction

This chapter outlines how carbon dioxide and, later on, shale gas became objects of energy politics in the context of EU membership. Each case is discussed separately but the common goal is to show how the making of these two objects involved various non-domestic actors and their particular interests. In this chapter, I seek to understand how the making of these two objects formed part of Orientalizing and de-Orientalizing discourses about Poland during the last three decades. In both stories, US-based actors were the first ones to introduce carbon dioxide and shale gas to the political agendas of the then ruling governments of Poland. However, in both cases, it was the EU that stabilized, or destabilized, their existence in relation to energy and climate politics and established itself as a reference point for the further discourses and actions of Polish actors in this area. As the story unfolds, one sees that the objectification of carbon dioxide and shale gas was politicized not only in Poland but also in Western Europe. This in turn shows that concerns about climate change and environmental impacts open energy-related issues up to broader political debate. As the analysis unfolds, it will become increasingly clear that energy politics in the age of climate change and environmental concerns can neither be held within a narrow frame of energy security and economic development nor constrained within the political domains of a nation state.

Making carbon dioxide into an object of energy politics: the pre-accession years

By the time the US-based think tank Environmental Defense Fund launched its campaign promoting emissions trade within the United Nations Framework Convention on Climate Change (UNFCCC), it had already approached environmental experts around the newly established government in Poland about the concept in the early 1990s. This was the first attempt to make carbon dioxide into an object of economic and political calculation in one of the post-socialist countries. As Tomasz Żylicz (2000) from the Warsaw Ecological Economics Centre points out, the year 1989 marked the beginning of a comprehensive reform of Poland's environmental policies. The newly established Economics Department of the Ministry of the Environment in Poland "strongly recommended taking advantage of emissions trading to improve the cost-effectiveness of the new policies" (Żylicz 2000, p. 141). The idea of emissions trading attracted the interest of a broad range of Polish actors, including academics, politicians and businesspeople, as it apparently resonated with the neo-liberal agenda of Poland's transformation designers and the ideas for environmental policy reform developed by dissident economists prior to 1989 (Żylicz 2000, p. 147). A potential political advantage of the tradable pollution permits (TPPs) identified by the dissident economists was that of "letting the market constrain the power of bureaucracies" (Żylicz 2000, p. 147), an appealing prospect in the context of the elite change and steering the political economy towards global markets. If put on the market, carbon dioxide could become a global commodity.

In 1991, the Polish Parliament officially approved the incorporation of TPPs into the National Environmental Policy. In the same year, a new Environmental Protection Act was drafted which included TPPs as a policy option. The policy framing was in place, with TPPs anchored into various legislative acts. However, despite this progress, environmental reforms slowed down and the 1991 bill was not passed (Żylicz 2000). The US inspiration was not a sufficient trigger; Polish elites looked up to Europe, and at that time Western European counterparts perceived TPPs as ethically ambiguous (Żylicz 2000). In Western Europe at the time, taxation and command-and-control policy tools dominated environmental debates, including the slowly emerging discussions on climate change. Be it a market-based or a command-and-control policy tool, carbon dioxide would embed into the political and economic lives of state and business actors in quite a different way. In a command-and-control system, each ton of carbon dioxide would constitute a cost measured with an administratively fixed tax rate. If put on the market, the price of carbon dioxide would be an effect of relations between sellers and buyers of permits for carbon dioxide and of the supply and demand for these certificates. In both systems, the rules of taxation as well as the rules of the markets would involve negotiations between business and state actors.

All these differences aside, it is important to realize that at this point Poland started to take emissions trade into consideration much more readily than the European Community. Can this be interpreted as backwardness or progressiveness? Can the interest in TPPs be seen as an Orientalizing or a de-Orientalizing move? It all depends on the perspective and the context. From the Western European perspective, a policy turn towards TPPs in Poland was seen as ethically ambiguous and "foreign" for Europe. It was an idea that came from the US and was spread by US-based actors to Eastern economies – not just to Poland but also, for example, to Kazakhstan. From the US perspective, yes, Polish economic and political systems were surely in need of solid reforms. Poland was part of the Orient from the point of view of the Western policy world. However, the US actors not only lobbied "the East", but they also approached the UNFCCC negotiation tables and, several years after the "Polish episode", successfully turned the cap-and-trade system into the main tool for greenhouse gas emission reductions under the Kyoto Protocol (1997). Moreover, at the beginning of the 2000s, the European Commission started to educate itself in the technicalities of cap-and-trade. Could Poland have become one of those actors teaching the European Commission based on its own experience? Would the East, the European Orient, have been able to help transform the West? Probably yes, if only the experiments in the early 1990s with TPPs (in other words, with cap-and-trade) had been successful. And the story that unfolds beneath this paragraph will show how it failed.

In the autumn of 1989 a Polish-American workshop took place at which TPPs were recommended to Poland's new democratic government. The US experts said that "even in thin or hardly existing markets, substantial cost savings could be achieved, if at least one low-cost polluter and a neighboring high-cost polluter were allowed to comply with certain regulations jointly" (Żylicz 2000, p. 148). For the first time, pollution, including carbon dioxide, was weighed and compared in terms of costs gains and framed as an object that could be traded between different power sector companies. An interesting assumption was made that a pre-existing infrastructure of a market for pollution was not necessary, as it would emerge and become more robust once a commodity started to be traded. In the late 1980s, "the central planning ideology has been severely eroded in Poland" (Żylicz 2000, p. 148). At the same time, however, institutional and organizational bases for constructing an emissions market were very weak. It soon became obvious that there were also some cognitive and psychological barriers to overcome, as industrial managers did not know how to operate on free markets for the goods they produced, let alone for the emissions

they generated. Industrial managers were used to the "excessive pater-
nalism of state administration" (Żylicz 2000, p. 148). Consequently,
Żylicz (2000) points to the absence of well-established market structures
and entrepreneurial behaviour as two vital obstacles for implementing
emissions trade in Poland in the early 1990s. Additionally, the implementation of emissions trade in Poland was hindered by the system of
pollution charges that already existed in Poland, having been established
in the 1980s. "The main challenge thus seemed not so much to depart
from command-and-control approaches, but rather to persuade policy-
makers and stakeholders that, under the particular circumstances in
Poland at the time, TPPs were a preferred alternative to the existing
pollution charges" (Żylicz 2000, p. 148).

However, it slowly became clear that markets would not simply
emerge out of commodity trade. Markets need institutions, organization and people who know how to operate on them (Fligstein 1996). At
the beginning of the 1990s, the Polish-American experts had no empirical proof to persuade Polish business and administration actors that
even in "thin and weak markets" emissions trade could still unleash
entrepreneurial behaviour in actors and generate savings (Żylicz 2000,
p. 150). Performativity of economic theories (see Callon and Muniesa
2005) about cap-and-trade systems did not occur. Such a proof thus
had to be created. In 1990, the Economics Department set out to look
for a good site to demonstrate that emissions trading works and, to
develop this project, reached an agreement with the Environmental
Defense Fund (EDF) to cooperate with them. Soon the project managers realized that the physical and technological characteristics of a
site were as important as the approval of the regional environmental
administration (Żylicz 2000, p. 151). One of the demonstration projects
was launched in Chorzów. However, no real emissions trading actually
took place there, since Polish law did not recognize emission reduction
credits as an economic entity. Pollution as an economic object, or its
equivalence in the form of a permit, did not exist.[1]

The other project was carried out in Opole with funding from the
EU pre-accession programme, the European "Poland and Hungary:
Assistance for the Restructuring of the Economy" (PHARE) programme. PHARE offered to finance a few full-scale research projects
addressing problems of practical importance for the Ministry of the
Environment. The Opole project was originally conceived of as an
implementation exercise for the EU ETS. However, with the political
establishment being only marginally interested in environmental policy
reforms, there was no opportunity for an appropriate amendment of
the legislation. "Consequently, the project was redesigned and, instead

of actual implementation, a series of computer simulations served as a test of the legal mechanism that needed to be developed" (Żylicz 2000, p. 154).

The third project to demonstrate the effectiveness of emissions trade was the Jadwisin workshop organized by the Polish Ministry of the Environment together with the Harvard Institute for International Development in June 1996. Its goal was

> to elucidate the relationship between tradability of permits and emerging European legislative issues ... The Workshop provided an opportunity to assess Polish plans to introduce emissions trading from the point of view of both US practical experience, and the European legal framework.
>
> (Żylicz 2000, p. 155)

The Directorate-General for Environment (DG Environment) of the European Commission presented "European issues" at the Jadwisin workshop. At that time, the Integrated Pollution and Prevention Control (IPPC) was the most important piece of legislation of the European environmental policy. Therefore, emissions trade was largely discussed in the context of Poland's preparation to transpose the IPPC rules to the Polish legislation. DG Environment officials made it clear that the IPPC Directive imposed some extra requirements on pollution sources, but it did not preclude emissions trading. Nevertheless, it was said that emissions trade could not overrule any source- and/or site-specific conditions that policy-makers in Europe were likely to retain. That was the moment when, despite the efforts of the US actors to implement emissions trading in Poland, the EU legislation overrode all previous plans, projects and discussions on the matter. Once Poland set out on the path to European integration, the European rules governing environmental protection began to take priority over the policy options coming from the US.

While the concept of emissions trading experienced its ups and downs in the US Senate and in the Polish government, Western European countries made a slow turn towards reducing carbon emissions. The European Union Emissions Trading System (EU ETS), which began to operate in the EU in 2005, stems from almost two decades of Western European thinking on how to translate emission reduction into an economic opportunity. The first attempts to reduce carbon dioxide emissions in Europe date back to the beginning of the 1990s. At that time, several countries came up with their own domestic targets and policies for reducing emissions. In 1989, the Dutch government issued its first National

Environmental Policy Plan (NEPP), which called for carbon dioxide emissions from the Netherlands to be stabilized at average 1989/1990 levels until the year 2000. In June 1990, the West German government announced a target of a 25–30 percent reduction in emissions compared to 1987 levels by 2005. In the same year the Danish government stated that it would reduce carbon dioxide emissions by 20 percent in relation to 1988 levels by 2005. The Austrian government followed these three countries with a goal of a 20 percent reduction in emissions compared to 1988 levels by 2005 (Schreus and Tiberghien 2007, p. 32). These efforts were soon taken up at the European Community level and, as early as October 1990, the European Ministers of Energy and the Environment declared that the European Community "would seek to stabilize its joint carbon dioxide emissions at 1990 levels by the turn of the century" (Schreus and Tiberghien 2007, p. 20). However, the three cohesion countries – Spain, Portugal and Greece – demanded a "burden-sharing" approach that would allow them to declare their own reduction goals corresponding to their lower levels of economic development.

A burden-sharing approach was also adopted by the European Community in the 1997 negotiations at the Kyoto Conference. It guaranteed success because it took into account economic differences between the involved economies. When the European Commission pushed for an ambitious community-wide target, it also recognized a need for differentiation in national targets. As a result, "only seven [member states] were expected to reduce their emissions: Austria, Belgium, Denmark, Germany, Italy, Luxemburg, the Netherlands, and the United Kingdom. Other EU member states either pledged to stabilize their emissions (Finland, France) or to work to reduce the rate at which they were growing (Spain, Greece, Portugal, Sweden, and Ireland)" (Schreus and Tiberghien 2007, p. 33). During the Kyoto negotiations, the EU committed itself to cutting 8 percent of its 1990 emissions in the period 2008–2012. The stepping down of the US Bush administration from the Kyoto negotiations at the beginning of the 2000s was a major blow for the global efforts to curb carbon emissions. However, for the EU it provided an opportunity for it to take up the role of the leader, the norm leader (Ellickson 2001, Hechter and Opp 2001, Lightfoot and Burchell 2005, Manners 2002) and a political entrepreneur (Tiberghien 2007), and to build up its image as a global guardian of the climate system.

It is worthwhile to examine why some member states declared such ambitious emission reduction targets at the beginning of the 1990s. Schreus and Tiberghien (2007) point to changing underlying economic conditions amongst the biggest member states (p. 32). Germany provides a good example of how the country's changing economic conditions were coined into an ambitious climate policy. Due to the collapse of many industries in the East of the newly unified Germany, the country as a whole experienced huge windfall reductions in carbon emissions. Later on, a strong position of the German Green Party, invited by the Social Democratic Party to join the coalition after the 1998 elections, resulted in a successful push for an ecological tax reform (reducing the tax burden on workers, while increasing it on energy consumption), a nuclear phase-out plan, the active promotion of renewable energies through special feed-in tariffs and an aggressive climate change policy (Schreus and Tiberghien 2007, p.37). The UK and France, on the other hand, provide good examples of how existing policies were conducive to ambitious emission reduction goals. The UK, which had been sceptical about emission reductions in the early 1990s, turned into a strong supporter of climate action when it started the switch from coal- to gas-fuelled power stations. Tony Blair, the then Prime Minister, established himself as a big supporter of climate action in order to improve his image as a politician independent from the US around the time of the Iraq War (Schreus and Tiberghien 2007, p. 38). France, whose carbon dioxide emissions are currently less than half those of Germany, achieved this level mainly due to its decision in the 1970s to become less dependent on energy imports. In 2007, 59 nuclear reactors produced 78 percent of the country's electricity and accounted for the bulk of the 50 percent energy autonomy boasted by France (Schreus and Tiberghien 2007, p. 39). According to Schreus and Tiberghien (2007), up until 2005 France played only a limited role in international climate negotiations. However, at a certain point its bureaucracy realized that "Kyoto can serve to buttress the role of technocratic elites, playing up their strengths in the nuclear and automobile sectors" (p. 39). Also, President Chirac seized upon climate change as a major political entrepreneurial issue. Smaller countries such as Austria, Belgium, Denmark, Finland, Luxemburg, the Netherlands and Sweden managed, on many occasions, to form a strong coalition pushing for climate change action. The Netherlands and Denmark in particular have been particularly strong advocates of emission reductions. The latter soon became a pioneer in developing renewable energies (Schreus and Tiberghien 2007, p. 39). Austria, on the other hand, had a strong environmental movement which pushed the government for action. All these policy decisions were being taken by original EU member states while Poland was still struggling with an economic and political transformation from socialism.

Poland signed the Climate Convention on 26 July 1994 and ratified the Kyoto Protocol on 13December 2002, making a commitment to reduce greenhouse gas emissions by 6 percent within the period 2008–2012 as compared to 1988 emission levels (Jankowski 2006). As Jankowski points out, these decisions were taken in Poland after a great deal of hesitation and discussion as to whether "the policy of reducing carbon dioxide emission would not impose too much of a burden on Poland, because of its hard coal domination in fuel consumption" (Jankowski 2006, p. 393). At that time, the European Commission was proposing a "carbon tax" which was the source of most concerns raised in coal-dependent Poland. However, as Jankowski (2006) sums up, "the political will to support the efforts of the international community on climate protection prevailed" (p. 393). What surely helped Poland to comply with the Kyoto targets was the collapse of many national industries followed by considerable reductions in carbon dioxide emissions. In fact, as early as 2001, Poland's emission reductions reached ten times the amount committed in Kyoto. In 1988 Poland's carbon dioxide emissions were 476.6 Mt and in 2001 they were 317.8 Mt (66.8 percent of the 1988 levels). The situation was similar to that in Germany where the collapse of East German industries resulted in emission reductions across the whole country. However, the main difference resided in the fact that Germany still had a rich, well-developed Western part of the country which was able to economically pull East Germany up and provide resources for investment there. Poland did not have a "rich Western part", so the social cost of the economic transition was very high and evenly spread across the whole country. In 2003, the unemployment rate in Poland reached 20 percent. Moreover, Poland's economic growth at that time was energy- and carbon-intensive, so it was difficult to accept the new principle of carbon dioxide emission reductions that came with EU accession (see Jankowski 2006), and catching up with the West economically was the main principle organizing various post-transition processes in the Polish economy (Buchowski 2017; Dunn 2008; Hann 2002), which was perceived as a difficult but worthy path. Any additional burdens imposed by the EU, neighbouring countries or other international organizations were thus seen by Polish economic and political actors as malign acts of sabotage on Poland's future prosperity.

More importantly, however, the collapse of its industries meant that carbon dioxide disappeared from the Polish economy without any need for a policy action or framing – be it cap-and-trade or command-and-control. It disappeared both as a commodity and as a taxable externality. Carbon dioxide, which vanished alongside the dismantled and abandoned industrial installations, was an object that did not constitute any visible challenge for business or political actors. Policy- and business-wise, it was a non-object. Politically and symbolically, it stood for the collapse of the Polish economy during the years of transition and for the loss of thousands of jobs. However, this symbolic framing was only explicated later, in 2008, after the European Commission had demanded the same efforts from both old and new EU member states. Between 2002 (the ratification of the Kyoto Protocol) and 2008 (amendments to the EU Emissions Trading System Directive) carbon dioxide survived in the life of Polish policy in a rudimentary form. Legislation necessary to comply with the Kyoto Protocol (1997) and the first ETS Directive (Directive 2003/87/EC) was implemented but, at the time, carbon dioxide was just a matter of administration. It was a technical issue, not a political one, it did not bother anyone too much and it did not trigger discussions that would go beyond the administration of carbon dioxide registries.

The historical experience of economic breakdown in the early 1990s and a feeling of entitlement to grow economically, and thus emit more, dominated Poland's discourse on carbon dioxide reduction for the next few decades. However, following EU accession in 2004, it was difficult to maintain this historically charged discourse. It was expected by European policy actors that the pre-accession years would have already brought some order to the Polish economy and fairly deeply de-Orientalized it into an already transitioned space. While the attempts made by the US actors to establish emission trade in Poland in the early 1990s came as part of a package of Orientalizing development discourses offered by Western neo-liberal reformists to a socialist economy, the EU climate policies of the 2000s did away with this discourse and tried to de-Orientalize Poland and subject it to equal, or fairly equal, treatment. In this new context, Polish actors sought to bring back Orientalizing discourses of development in order to self-Orientalize in a pre-emptive way. Further examples of such attempts will be presented in Chapter 3, in which the 2008 Climate Change and Energy Package debate in the EU will be discussed. For now, it suffices to say that the collapse of many industries in Poland and the huge reductions in carbon dioxide emissions that happened "on the way to a painful economic transition" will be repeatedly mobilized by Polish actors to take Poland out of EU and global climate change policy regimes.

Making carbon dioxide into an object of energy politics: post-accession EU years

In May 2004, Poland joined the EU and thus also the EU Emissions Trading System (EU ETS), established with the 2003 EU ETS Directive. According to the directive, the first trading period would start in 2005 and end in 2007, and the Polish government was obliged to prepare a National Allocation Plan (NAP), which would list all the companies participating in the EU ETS and the amount of emission allowances (EU Allowances, or EUAs) that each company would be granted for this trading period. The work on the Polish NAP started relatively late, in December 2003 (see Jankowski 2006). From Jankowski's (2006) point of view, integration of new EU members into the EU ETS "was made in the simplest way possible" (p. 397). The system designed for the original member states (the EU15) was automatically extended to new members and this was done "in spite of the fact that under Article 30 the Commission was obliged to consider and to outline 'how to adapt the Community scheme to an enlarged European Union'" (Jankowski 2006, p. 397). Jankowski (2006) also argues that "the situation and specific features of new EU members were not considered during the design of EU ETS" (p. 397). This resulted in "doubts regarding legal fundamentals and economic efficiency of this system" (Jankowski 2006, p. 397).

In short, Poland perceived the EU ETS as an administrative burden and an additional cost to the economy (still) in transition. EU ETS was also seen as being redundant due to the fact that in the middle of the first decade of the 2000s, despite its economic growth, Poland was still over-complying with its Kyoto emission reduction targets by 30 percent. Therefore, in the eyes of the Polish governmental and business actors there was simply no justification for Poland's participation in the ETS, if the only rationale behind it was to ensure compliance with the Kyoto targets of the EU as a regional organization. However, the Polish elites of that time did not consider the fact that the European elites had an ambitious plan to turn the EU into a global leader in climate change action and would not be stopped by just one of the member states. However, the economic interests of some EU member states and some companies bound by climate action remained fairly obscure for the Polish actors. With time, many actors from the power sector developed a narrative about German interests being behind the EU's climate action and the European model of energy transition (Heinrich 2018; Szulecki 2018).

Eventually, the Polish NAP was designed in such a way as to be able to take into account both the rules applied by the European Commission and Poland's economic and social situation (Jankowski 2006, p. 398). Many questions emerged regarding "the legitimacy of adaptation to disadvantageous EU ETS rules", given that Poland had "put in a lot of effort earlier, considerably reducing the emissions of CO_2" (p. 398) and had met the Kyoto Protocol limits. Therefore, the following rule was accepted as a fundamental guideline for the work on the Polish

NAP: "the implementation of EU ETS in Poland should not worsen the situation of the Polish economy compared to the situation of individual implementation of the Kyoto Protocol targets" (Jankowski 2006, p. 399). The main task of preparing the NAP was given over to the Ministry of the Environment, representatives of industry sectors covered by the ETS and independent experts (consultants). Jankowski (2006) observes that the Ministry of the Economy played a more minor role, which was criticized by industries. There was, however, "a common conviction that CO_2 emissions and ETS are a big issue for the old EU countries, not for Poland" (Jankowski 2006, p. 399). In this debate, Polish actors Orientalized the Polish economy themselves, as they did not want to see it as part of the Western economic system. According to Jankowski (2006), "at a relatively early phase of the work, the Ministry of Environment decided to propose additional bonuses above emission projections in order to acknowledge early action" (p. 400).

On 22 December 2004, the Polish Parliament adopted legislation regulating emissions trading in Poland, which emphasized the economic efficiency of emission reductions. Most of the legislative acts regulating emissions trading and the allocation of emission allowances came relatively late, in 2005, 2006 and 2007. This together with the incompetence of local officials and inadequate emissions measurement techniques resulted in low efficiency of emissions trading in Poland. There were also huge delays in reporting and verifying yearly emissions by particular installations. Verification could only be carried out by certified auditors, who in 2005–2006 were still very scarce on the Polish market. As Regulski (2008) points out, the auditing companies that operated in Poland at that time offered their services at extremely high prices, which deterred smaller businesses from being able to use them. On the other hand, provincial officials entitled to do the auditing lacked the required training and resources necessary to carry out the task. The National Registry of Allowances was only established in July 2006, meaning that actual emissions trading was delaying until that time. All of this resulted in many companies losing opportunities for financial gain, as they were unable to start emissions trading in 2005 (Regulski 2008). The question thus is whether self-Orientalization was only a discursive strategy of political elites towards the European elites or whether it was embedded in the everyday functioning of state institutions. Consequently, the collapse of the ETS in 2007, when the price of EUAs hit its lowest price of €0.03 in December 2007, deprived Polish companies of any chances of making a profit on the ETS during the first trading period, 2005–2007. In addition, while many foreign companies learned how to use other Kyoto mechanisms (e.g., the Clean Development and the Joint

Implementation Mechanisms), Polish companies were still struggling with slow and incompetent institutions.

As latecomers to the EU ETS and with a self-Orientalizing view of their own position within it, Polish actors were thus not able to make any profit from this scheme. They did not know how to deal with the new object – carbon dioxide turned into a commodity. A lost opportunity to learn how to trade emissions offered by the US actors during the transition years was also a lost lesson for the post-accession emissions trading. The EU institutions and other EU member states started to learn how to benefit from the system in the years when Poland was struggling with its transitional reforms, including privatization and fiscal and social reforms. During the pre-accession negotiations, climate policies were not of prime importance to the CEE accession countries. Negotiating agricultural policies and access to the EU's structural funds were seen as much more important for the Polish government. Climate policies and their difficult emissions reduction processes were seen in Poland as a problem faced by Western countries. It was not on the minds of the CEE governments, and surely not on the minds of Poland's political and economic leaders. As Chapter 3 will show, this had to change radically within the space of one year, 2008, when the European Commission proposed new stricter rules for the ETS.

Making shale gas into an object of energy politics

Shale gas, although physically trapped in the shale rock formations in the territory of Poland for hundreds of thousands of years, had never before become an issue of political or economic debate as it did in the 2010s. It had never been there as a thing, an object relevant to energy politics. In the archives of the Polish Geological Institute (PGI) are stored data from as early as the 1970s that give a rough assessment of the volumes of hydrocarbons in Polish shale plate, but these data had never before mobilized the Polish government or oil and gas companies to act. The push for a transformation of its status to objectification came from an external source, the US Energy Information Agency, which in 2011 published a report assessing shale gas reserves globally, including in Poland (EIA 2011). The EIA (2011) report, titled *World Shale Gas Resources: An Initial Assessment of 14 Regions Outside the United States* provided a trigger for launching shale oil and gas exploration not only in Poland, but also in China and Argentina. According to the study, Polish shale resources could be among the largest in Europe, right after France. We can interpret this as an Orientalizing moment in the history of post-socialist, post-accession Poland, similar to the one we saw regarding carbon dioxide at the beginning of the 1990s. Due to the EIA (2011) report, Poland's economy, in particular its subterranean geological spaces, once again became interesting and potentially exploitable for Western actors. Poland's subsoil was a potential space for Western (specifically US) intervention that could bring a profit. Western actors with strong invested interests included powerful and resourceful upstream oil and gas companies with large portfolios of extraction projects all over the world. Very early on, after the publication of the EIA (2011) report, the US government established contact between the US Geological Survey (USGS) and Polish state agencies and companies. One of the experts from the USGS spent over a year working with the US Embassy in Warsaw, doing "geological diplomacy" in Poland and organizing knowledge exchange about technical, economic and political issues related to shale gas extraction. In other words, Poland once again came within the orbit of US interests. It was an area interesting to be around, learn about and develop alongside major US corporate interests.

However, the other EU member states were not so eager to become terrains for shale gas exploitation. The green movement and a nuclear lobby in France pushed unconventional hydrocarbons out of the domestic energy landscape. The French ban on fracking positioned French anti-fracking activists quite centrally in a growing global movement against this technology, even if it did not prevent French companies such as Total from exploiting the resource elsewhere, for example in Argentina. Some other EU member states followed in the footsteps of the French government: The Bulgarian government banned fracking in 2012, and Germany and the UK followed this up with the introduction of moratoriums on using hydraulic fracturing technology for industrial purposes. Bans and moratoriums were also introduced in a number of US states (including North Carolina, New York, New Jersey, and Vermont, and more than 100 local governments) and in some other parts of the world (e.g. South Africa, Quebec in Canada and New South Wales in Australia) (Sonik 2012).

Despite these movements coming from inside the EU, the Polish government did not for one second consider imposing a ban on fracking. It wanted the resource not only on paper but also in the pipelines. It was ready to turn it into an object of trade, into a commodity. And, as the story unfolds below, the Polish government strove to do this at a time when shale gas had not yet been established as an object in energy politics globally and was non-existent in Europe. Moreover, while the Polish government and some oil and gas companies tried to objectify it and stabilize it in the European context, many European actors, such citizens' groups or NGOs, attempted to destabilize it, to question its place in energy politics at large. From 2007, the Ministry of the Environment began granting licences for shale gas exploration, reaching 113 in number by 2010. More than 23 companies obtained permits, including national, partially state-owned and international players. Most licences belonged to Polish state-owned companies: PGNiG S.A. (15), Orlen Upstream Sp. z o.o. (9) and Lotos Petrobaltic S.A. (8). Foreign companies, including some global giants, owned between one and five licences each: Chevron (4), MarathonOil (4), Total (1) and ExxonMobil (1). Permits were issued for a period of five years and some licence holders chose not to apply for an extension, likely a result of unfavourable geological conditions in some areas or the poor financial standing of some companies, in addition to unclear policy plans of the Polish government (Sawicki 2014a, 2014b).

The report of the EIA (2011) caused what is identified in human geography literature as "resource affect" (Weszkalnys 2016), which is understood "both as an intrinsic element of capitalist dynamics and as an object problematized by corporate, government, and third-sector practice" (p. 127). Shale gas was, at that time, still not a resource in any physical sense, but it very quickly became an important object of resource politics in Poland, as well as a thing desired to be physically objectified. Images of great prosperity and economic growth, with slogans such as "Poland will become the second Kuwait" or "the second Norway" evoked visions of prosperity and rapid economic development – finally (sic!) catching up with the West. This view was not only popular among political and business elites but also among Polish citizens (Wagner 2017; Lis and Stankiewicz 2017; CBOS 2013), as the gains from shale gas extraction were supposed to trickle down to society as a whole. The Prime Minister at the time, Donald Tusk, heralded the opening of a National Wealth Fund which would in the future finance pensions for all citizens and public healthcare. But the promise that was expressed most strongly by the Polish political elites concerned the possibility of enhancing Poland's energy security by becoming less dependent on, and maybe even completely free of, Russian gas supplies (Lis 2018). Resource affect is a significant part of resource-making politics. Discursive framing positions the future object in relation to other objects and to other political realms and visions, such as energy security, modernization, economic development and intergenerational prosperity. It opens up broad horizons for envisioning the future – ultimate de-Orientalization as in the Polish case – and triggers collective images that go beyond the technicalities of energy politics.

Prospects of resource extraction also bring about what Weszkalnys (2016) calls a "doubtful hope", because they evoke images of potential conflicts and frictions caused by extraction processes and the appearance of the resource – the physical object – in geopolitical relations. In the studied case of the Polish shale gas effect, although the overall vision was so overwhelmingly positive, it soon became mixed with fear. The fear congealed in various formulations of threats uttered by governmental actors and was induced by the real or alleged activities of various actors, including the Russian energy giant Gazprom, the European Commission, the European Parliament or anti-fracking activists. In this context, shale gas was transformed from an economic object – a resource – into a political one – a resource that would guarantee Poland's energy security but also an object that would trigger political conflicts. These mixed hopes and fears resulted in a decision to consider shale gas an issue of Poland's foreign policy and to engage the Ministry of Foreign Affairs to speak on behalf of the Polish government about it with the EU and with partners from the US and Canada (Lis 2018). The Ministry of Foreign Affairs established a narrative that positioned shale gas within a wider context of security concerns (Lis 2018).

The narrative which was exposed the most had the aim of envisioning a future without Russian gas supplies. Historically, a solid ground was established for this hope to capture the imagination of the wider public of Polish citizens. Their shared hopes were reflected in different opinion polls about the perceived benefits of shale gas extraction (CBOS 2013). In the first decade of the twenty-first century, Poland was reliant on Russian gas supplies for about 60 percent of its total gas consumption, although this dependency has steadily been falling in the last couple of years. In September 2005, Gazprom signed an agreement with its German partners, E.ON Ruhrgas and BASF, to construct a 1,200-kilometre-long pipeline of a total capacity of 55 billion cubic metres per year between the Russian town of Vyborg and Ludmil, near Greifswald in Germany, running below the Baltic Sea (Heinrich 2018). The pipeline was named North Stream and it aroused a strong political reaction from subsequent Polish governments. It was negatively stigmatized in public as "the second Ribbentrop–Molotow pact" and identified as a potential threat to the security of Russian gas supplies in the future. For the Polish political elites, it became clear that Poland was no longer perceived as a transfer country for Russian gas supplies. And even if, as a consequence of the Ukrainian-Russian conflicts in 2005–2006, 2009 and 2014–2015, the Russians were blaming and shaming not Poland but the Ukraine and its political elites for every interruption in gas transfer to Europe, the North Stream project was framed in Poland as a political act to erase Poland from the gas transfer maps (see Heinrich

2018). Therefore, the main fear, which turned the "shale gas hope" into the "shale gas doubtful hope", was that at some point Russia might somehow spoil Poland's shale gas plans and shatter its dream of gas independence from Russia (see also Wagner 2017; Upham et al. 2015). The Russian-Ukrainian conflict only helped to strengthen this discourse, and when the Polish Prime Minister Donald Tusk presented a project of the European Energy Union in the opinion section of the *Financial Times*, titled *A united Europe can end Russia's energy stranglehold* (Tusk 2014), he mentioned shale gas as a viable option for enhancing the energy security of the EU as a whole. The Russian-Ukrainian conflict and the growing concerns of EU officials about the security of gas supplies to the whole of the EU was the moment when the stabilization of shale gas as an object of EU energy politics seemed most possible to achieve.

The article in the *Financial Times* shows that although the US actors introduced shale gas into Poland's energy politics as a strategic object, the Polish government and companies quickly began to orient their activities onto the EU arena as a viable source of constraints and opportunities. This makes the case of shale gas objectification similar to the one mentioned before about carbon dioxide. The Ministry of Foreign Affairs cooperated with Polish Members of the European Parliament (MEPs) and with the Brussels-based representation office of PGNiG, the biggest oil and gas company in Poland, to lobby for a more positive attitude to unconventional fossil fuels in Europe and against any attempts to introduce stricter environmental regulations in that area (Lis 2018). One of the fears was that climate-sensitive EU officials would ban fracking or introduce harsh regulations for the sake of keeping that particular fossil fuel underground. This was the moment when the political lives of two objects crossed paths: carbon dioxide as a well-stabilized object of climate and energy politics of the EU may have pushed shale gas off the EU's energy agenda as being a carbon-intensive fossil fuel. According to the information from the Ministry itself, the first governmental note about shale gas was written by a staff member in the Ministry of Foreign Affairs in 2009 (Interview 1). Led by Radosław Sikorski, the Ministry worked to popularize the view that shale gas development in the US could be replicated in Europe with positive consequences for the economy and security of supply. The Ministry cooperated with Polish companies and international companies operating in Poland, and was involved in various negotiation and lobbying activities in the EU until the start of 2014 when the European Commission issued the Communication on Exploration and Production of Hydrocarbons (2014/70/EU) (Interview 1).

Between 2011 and 2016, a pro-fracking lobby in the EU became almost unequivocally associated with Polish governmental and business actors. An assistant of a Polish MEP told me, during an interview at his Brussels' office, that right from the very start of the debate on shale gas in Brussels this issue was perceived as "the Polish issue" (Interview 2). When the European Parliament was required to vote on two shale gas related reports – the report of the Environmental (ENVI) Committee led by Bogus Sonik (a Polish MEP) and the Industry (ITRE) Committee led by Niki Tzavela (a Green MEP) – the Polish delegation to the EU, in cooperation with PGNiG, organized an exhibition at the European Parliament called "Shale Gas for Europe". The exhibition was vehemently criticized by the European Greens and by the community of NGOs in Brussels, who claimed that the Polish actors had broken the rules of acceptable lobbying at the Parliament. They issued a complaint to the Secretariat of the European Parliament and, as a result, PGNiG were banned from attending the European Parliament for half a year.

Looking at these attempts in a more theoretical way, Orientalized by the US actors and de-Orientalized as part of the EU, Polish actors tried to carve out their own strategy in relation to shale gas within the EU institutions. Contrary to the case of carbon dioxide emissions, this time Polish actors tried to influence policy processes from within the EU. Several MEPs actively shaped the work of the committees of the European Parliament. PGNiG's lobbying, although counter-productive in some respects, was directed at influencing the EU debate at large. However, a real agenda-setting move was made by Donald Tusk, the then ruling Prime Minister of Poland, who formulated the pillars of the Energy Union in the above-mentioned *Financial Times* editorial (Tusk 2014). Later on, a non-paper was written by the staff members of his cabinet:

> The EU should also support those Member States which decided to exploit their unconventional gas and oil resources by: emphasizing the fundamental importance of unconventional resources for the EU's security of supply and competitiveness; confirming that current EU legislation is adequate and sufficient for the safe exploitation of unconventional resources so there is no need for new legislative proposals in this respect; stressing that drafting specific national regulations on environmental and investment conditions (i.e. for the extraction of shale gas) lies within the competence of Member States; supporting the integration of shale gas infrastructure with the gas networks of Member States; supporting the development of environmentally safe unconventional hydrocarbon

technologies, sharing best practices and raising public awareness (e.g. under HORIZON 2020).

(Ministry of Foreign Affairs 2014, p. 8)

The Polish government firmly occupied the position that no new regulations were needed, as there already existed enough European legislative acts on environmental protection, monitoring or water use. Consequently, Polish MEPs blocked amendments to the Environmental Impact Assessment Directive proposed by the European Parliament in 2013 that would have impeded the development of the unconventional hydrocarbons industry. Simultaneously, they sent a clear message to the European Commission that a new directive dedicated to unconventional hydrocarbons was not welcomed by the Polish government of the time. The Polish position on shale gas in the EU was being developed strictly in relation to the idea of a European Energy Union. An official from the Brussels-based office of the Polish Representation in the EU, in conversation with me, commented on the role that shale gas could play for the energy security of Poland. He drew a broad picture of several member states being dependent on a single gas supplier – six of which were 100 percent dependent on one supplier, Gazprom. According to the Polish official, irrespective of the way in which the Energy Union was going to develop, shale gas was supported by the Polish government as one of the solutions to external dependencies of European countries on foreign gas supplies (Interview 3).

Therefore, by inscribing shale gas extraction into the idea of Energy Union, Polish political actors tried to propose an energy object that would not only be useful for their domestic energy policy but that would also enhance energy security for the whole of the EU. They tried to scale it up, to turn it from an object vital for Polish energy politics into an object important for the EU as a whole. While the first framing came with the US EIA Report (2011) and with an Orientalizing agenda of resource extraction by Western global corporations, the latter came as a result of interactions and relations established within the EU political arena. The latter should certainly be seen as a de-Orientalizing move, one that tried to establish shale gas as a European issue and relate it to European debates on energy efficiency. And this move did not seem so desperate after all, given that not all EU institutions thought that keeping that resource underground would be for the best. The DG Environment and DG Industry took opposing positions on that issue. While the DG Environment expressed concern about the climate and the environmental impacts of shale gas extraction, the DG Energy was eager to give the shale gas project a chance as a potential trigger for economic growth in Europe. In addition, the European Parliament was not unequivocal in that respect. In 2011, the European Parliament's Committee on Environment, Public Health and Food Safety commissioned a report on "Impacts of shale gas and shale oil extraction on the environment and on human health" (Lechtenböhmer et al. 2011). The report covered a wide range of impacts: water, soil, earthquakes, chemicals, radioactivity and impacts on human health. It also addressed the problem of greenhouse gas emissions and, more specifically, the role of shale gas production for long-term reductions of carbon dioxide emissions. The authors of the report predicted that "assuming environmental restrictions to increase costs and to reduce the speed of developments, shale gas production in Europe will remain almost marginal" (Lechtenböhmer et al. 2011, p. 76). An exception was made for Poland, where it was predicted that "here, it might have a visible impact as the low present production of 4.1 bcm covers about 30% of the low domestic demand of 13.7 bcm" (Lechtenböhmer et al. 2011, p. 76). At the same time, the report concluded that "existing mining laws in Europe and related regulations affecting mining activities do not take care of the specific aspects of hydraulic fracturing" (Lechtenböhmer et al. 2011, p. 77). Some of the details included in the recommendations were not received with satisfaction by Polish politicians and industry actors, especially the one stating that "an environmental impact assessment with public participation should be mandatory for each well" (Lechtenböhmer et al. 2011, p. 78). If implemented, this rule could substantially slow down development of the shale industry. Moreover, the authors of the report supported the idea that regional authorities should be more autonomous in deciding where to ban shale extraction. It was also assumed that, despite a growing demand for shale gas in Europe, Europe's internal production would further decrease and Europe would in any case need to increase imports from outside the EU. This attitude was a let-down for the Polish actors who saw shale gas extraction as a way to reduce reliance on Russian gas supplies.

The Poland-Brussels interactions were thus focused around making shale gas into an energy object or erasing it from energy policy debates. One important dimension that the Brussels actors brought into the shale gas debate was environmental and climate protection. Had it not been for the EU structures, the Polish actors would not have made much effort to relate shale gas exploration to environmental or climate impacts. As Chapter 4 will show, the environmental impacts of shale gas extraction were mainly studied because of the questions posed by the

the Brussels actors. It was also Brussels that helped to establish a relation between the burning of shale gas to produce energy in Europe and carbon dioxide emissions. Some environmental groups, such as Food and Water Watch Europe, did not want any shale gas to be extracted from the European subsoil as they did not want to see any more fossil fuels in European energy production systems. Because of this, it was difficult to secure a solid place for shale gas in the EU, even if only in its main policy arena in Brussels. It was an unwanted object for many actors there, an object that should be primarily framed in relation to its environmental and climate impacts. These actors usually opposed any propositions for economic framing. avFor the Polish actors, however, enchanted by the hope of becoming less dependent on Russian gas supplies, the economic and security framing were crucial. However, as Chapter 4 will show, in order to turn shale gas into a resource and thereby insert it into economic systems, a lot of below-ground industrial activities had to be undertaken. And these activities demanded capital.

Conclusions

As the analysis has shown, neither carbon dioxide nor shale gas were ready-made objects with a fixed framing and an ontological status for different actors. The exact point at which their presence was first felt in Polish energy politics cannot be precisely determined, though there are events that we can bring in in order to understand the twists and turns of the story. My goal in this chapter was to highlight the various relational processes through which both entities were gaining their ontological status not only in the context of energy, but also of climate and politics, and not only in Poland, but also in EU as a whole. The statuses of carbon dioxide and shale gas were far from being stable, or given once and for good; they were constantly being negotiated and re-negotiated by various actors with different agendas. The following chapters will reveal more details about these negotiations, about finding the right place for Polish carbon dioxide on the EU ETS and about the struggles to develop shale gas extraction in Poland and ensure that it could not be de-materialized by EU regulations.

Note

1 In 1991, a new Environmental Protection Act was drafted by the government. It included Article 45, which stated that "the terms of a pollution permit can be transferred (either fully or in part) to another plant subject to the approval of the authority who issued the original permit". The Act

was eventually abandoned, so no emission reduction credits could formally become a commodity. Consequently, the whole experiment can be labelled as a "tradable permit project" only in a metaphorical sense (Żylicz 2000, p. 151).

References

Buchowski, M. (2017) *Czyściec: Antropologia Neoliberalnego Postsocjalizmu. [Anthropology of Neoliberal Post-Socialism].* Poznań: Wydawnictwo Naukowe UAM.

Callon M. and Muniesa, F. (2005) Economic markets as calculative collective devices. *Organizational Studies* 26(8): 1229–1250.

Centre for Public Opinion Research (CBOS). (2013) Społeczny stosunek do gazu łupkowego. Public opinion research conducted in May 2013. Warszawa: Fundacja Centrum Badania Opinii Społecznej. Retrieved 1 October 2013 from www.cbos.pl/SPISKOM.POL/2013/K_076_13.PDF

Dunn, E. (2008) *Prywatyzując Polskę. O bobofrutach, wielkim biznesie I rekonstrukcji pracy.* Warszawa: Wydawnictwo Krytyki Politycznej.

Energy Information Administration (EIA) (2011) *World Shale Gas Resources: An Initial Assessment of 14 Regions Outside the United States.* Retrieved 14 January 2014 from www.eia.gov/analysis/studies/worldshalegas/archive/2011/pdf/fullreport.pdf

Ellickson, R. C. (2001) The market of social norms. *American Law and Economics Review* 3(1):1–49.

Fligstein, N. (1996) Markets as politics: a political cultural approach to market institutions. *American Sociological Review* 61: 656–673.

Hann, C. (2002) Farewell to the socialist "Other". In: C. Hann (ed.), *Postsocialism: Ideas, Ideologies and Practices in Eurasia.* London: Routledge, pp. 1–11.

Hechter, M. and Opp, K.-D. (2001) *Social Norms.* New York: Russell Sage Foundation.

Heinrich, A. (2018) Securitization in the gas sector: energy security debates concerning the example of the Nord Stream Pipeline. In: K. Szulecki (ed.), *Energy Security in Europe: Divergent Perceptions and Policy Challenges.* Cham: Palgrave Macmillan, pp. 61–93.

Jankowski, B. (2006) Chapter 12: Poland. In: D. A. Ellerman, B. K. Buchner and C. Carraro (eds.), *Allocation in the European Emission Trading Scheme: Rights, Rents and Fairness.* Cambridge: Cambridge University Press, pp. 393–437.

Lechtenböhmer, S. et al. (2011) *Impacts of Shale Gas and Shale Oil Extraction on the Environment and on Human Health.* Retrieved from www.europarl.europa.eu/meetdocs/2009_2014/documents/envi/dv/shale_gas_pe464_425_final_/shale_gas_pe464_425_final_en.pdf

Lightfoot, S. and Burchell, J. (2005) The European Union and the World Summit on Sustainable Development: Normative Power Europe in action? *Journal of Common Market Studies* 43(1): 75–95.

Lis, A. (2018) Politics and knowledge production: between securitization and riskification of the shale gas issue in Poland and Germany. In: K. Szulecki (ed.), *Energy Security in Europe: Divergent Perceptions and Policy Challenges.* London: Palgrave Macmillan, pp. 93–116.

Lis, A. and Stankiewicz, P. (2017) Framing shale gas for policy-making in Poland. *Journal of Environmental Policy and Planning* 19(1): 53–71.

Manners, I. (2002) Normative Power Europe: a contradiction in terms? *Journal of Common Market Studies* 40(2): 235–258.

Regulski, B. (2008) *Zarządzanie uprawnieniami do emisji CO2 w przedsiębiorstwach ciepłowniczych w świetle KPRU na lata 2008–2012 [Management of carbon dioxde emission allowances in the heat production industries in the light of KPRU for 2008–2012].* Retrieved 10 April 2009 from http://archiwum.igcp. pl/system/files/1371_1323_Zarzadzanie_emisjami_i_uprawnieniami_do_ emisji_CO2_wobec_KPRU_II_0.pdf

Schreus, M. A. and Tiberghien, Y. (2007) Multi-level reinforcement: explaining European Union leadership in climate change mitigation. *Global Environmental Politics* 7(4): 19–46.

Szulecki, K. (ed.) (2018) *Energy Security in Europe: Divergent Perceptions and Policy Challenges.* London: Palgrave Macmillan.

Tiberghien, Y. (2007) *Entrepreneurial States: Reforming Corporate Governance in France, Japan, and Korea.* Ithaca, NY: Cornell.

Upham, P., Lis, A., Riesch, H. and Stankiewicz, P. (2015) Addressing social representations in socio-technical transitions with the case of shale gas. *Environmental Innovation and Societal Transitions.* 16: 120–141.

Wagner, A. (ed.) (2017) *Visible and Invisible: Nuclear Energy, Shale Gas and Wind Power in the Polish Media Discourse.* Kraków: Jagiellonian University Press.

Weszkalnys, G. (2016) A doubtful hope: resource affect in a future oil economy. *Journal of the Royal Anthropological Institute* 22: 127–146.

Żylicz, T. (2000) Obstacles of implementing tradable pollution permits: the case of Poland. In: OECD (ed.), *Implementing Domestic Tradable Permits for Environmental Protection (OECD Proceedings).* Paris: OECD Publishing, pp. 147–167.

Documents

Directive 2003/87/EC of the European Parliament and of the Council of October 2003 establishing a scheme for greenhouse gas emission allowance trading within the Community and amending Council Directive 96/61/EC, *Official Journal of the European Union*, 25 October 2003.

Kyoto Protocol (1997) UNFCCC. Retrieved 10 July 2018 from https://unfccc. int/resource/docs/convkp/kpeng.pdf

Ministry of Foreign Affairs (2014) Roadmap towards an Energy Union for Europe: Non-paper addressing the EU's energy dependency challenges. Retrieved 10 April 2018 from https://energypost.eu/wp-content/uploads/2014/ 05/2014-04-15-Roadmap-towards-Energy-Union_EN-the-PL-proposal.pdf

Sonik, B. (2012) Report on the environmental impacts of shale gas and shale oil extraction activities. European Parliament: Committee on the Environment, Public Health and Food Safety, 2011/2308(INI). Retrieved 14 April 2015 from www.europarl.europa.eu/sides/getDoc.do?pubRef=-//EP//NONSGML+REPORT+A7-2012-0283+0+DOC+PDF+V0//EN

Media reports

Sawicki, B. (2014a) Coraz mniej zainteresowanych łupkowymi koncesjami. *Łupki Polskie*. Retrieved 10 April 2014, from http://gazlupkowy.pl/coraz-mniej-zainteresowanych-lupkowymi-koncesjami/

Sawicki, B. (2014b) Sawicki: Dyskusja o NOKE powro'ci. *BiznesAlert*. Retrieved 10 April 2014 from http://biznesalert.pl/sawicki-dyskusja-o-noke-powroci/

Tusk, D. (2014) A united Europe can end Russia's energy stranglehold. *Financial Times* (21 April 2014). Retrieved 3 July 2014 from www.ft.com/intl/cms/s/0/91508464-c661-11e3-ba0e-00144feabdc0.html#axzz3C959I3vZ

Interviews

Interview 1: Expert at the Ministry of Foreign Affairs, Warsaw, May 2015.

Interview 2: MEP assistant, Brussels, June 2015.

Interview 3: Expert at the Permanent Representation of the Republic of Poland, Brussels, September 2015.

2 Production of expertise, scaling and carbon dioxide in Poland

Introduction

The story of how carbon dioxide became an economic and political object in Poland continued following amendments proposed by the European Commission in January 2008 to the EU Emissions Trading System (EU ETS) Directive (Directive 2003/87/EC) as part of the Climate Change and Energy Package (European Commission 2001). The Commission's proposal proved to be a wake-up call for CEE countries, especially for coal-dependent Poland, as it meant that carbon dioxide emissions would constitute an additional production cost, especially for electricity producers. Four years after its EU accession in 2004, Poland was still a new member state learning how to negotiate within the EU arena. A highly technical issue, the EU ETS for carbon dioxide was difficult to frame in economic and political terms. The 2008–2009 negotiations were thus accompanied by intensive efforts to produce expertise to help member states better understand the potential impacts of the changing system. Carbon dioxide emissions soon became an object functioning in various configurations of actors and in various assemblages (Callon and Muniesa 2005), within which its value was viewed differently. Depending on the proposed rules for the allocation of emission allowances, carbon dioxide was either a Polish, a European, a CEE or a Russian object. It was sometimes objectified as carbon dioxide emissions from coal and sometimes from gas, or from electricity production or industrial production. Some types of carbon dioxide emissions were seen as prone to "leaking" from Europe and some were seen as difficult to eliminate. And even though, as a chemical substance, carbon dioxide was still the same carbon dioxide, these different categories of carbon dioxide emissions were politically and economically very different.

As the story unfolds in this chapter, it becomes apparent that while fighting for their interests in the EU, Polish actors had to reflect on their own position in relation to other actors. Poland's first reaction to the proposal was to ask for an opt-out from the full auctions of EUAs for electricity producers. This was a self-Orientalizing move accompanied by different narratives about Poland as a space undergoing economic development, an economy "still in transition", a society "catching up with the West". However, this was not an effective discursive strategy in the European policy arena, as self-Orientalizing discourses do not work well among European policy actors. Values such as solidarity, Europeanness, common interests and perspectives are cherished in Brussels. For these reasons, Polish actors needed to think beyond "Polish carbon dioxide" and to look for broader categories for this awkward object and upscale their alternative policy options. However, after establishing alliances with German power producers and European industries, Polish actors were seen by many other actors in Brussels as playing the wrong game. Environmental NGOs openly accused the Polish government of not caring for its citizens, and instead supporting strong Western, mostly German, corporations in the power sector.

Europeanization of carbon dioxide emissions

In January 2008, the European Commission proposed a package of directives, known as the Climate Change and Energy Package, which included proposed amendments to the ETS Directive (European Commission 2001). The central aim of the reform was to subject electricity-producing companies to auctions of emission permits (EUAs) to cover their total carbon dioxide emissions from 2013 onwards. For industries the rule was different. The total amount of auctioned EUAs would depend on an industry-specific benchmark. In other words, some carbon dioxide emissions would still be free. These amendments were widely accepted in the EU, but not in Poland. The reason for this was simple. At the time, around 90 percent of Polish electricity was produced from coal (hard coal and lignite), which meant that the cost of almost every megawatt hour (MWh) of electricity produced in Poland would include the cost of carbon dioxide emissions. The time when Polish electricity producers could emit carbon dioxide for free was over. There was no longer any place for cheap carbon dioxide in the EU. The European Commission wanted to design an emissions market where one tonne of carbon dioxide emissions would cost around 30 euros.

Polish opposition to the new ideas coming from Brussels formed gradually. From January to June 2008, the Polish government was still busy constructing NAPs to comply with the previous version of the ETS Directive from 2003. At the end of August 2008, an expert in energy systems from the Warsaw Technical University was appointed by a group of energy-intensive industries and four power sector companies in Poland to work as a lobbyist in Brussels on their behalf. In the meantime, the Polish energy think tank EnergSys prepared the Report 2030 (EnergSys 2008) which countered the European Commission's calculations of the economic impacts of the reformed ETS on EU member states. The Polish report made assessments for Poland. The main difference between the two documents resided in the fact that while the Commission calculated the impacts of the ETS Directive on "an average EU economy" (European Commission 2008), the Report 2030 focused on the extreme Polish case. The results were very different (see Table 2.1 for details). The Commission foresaw an average increase in electricity prices across the 27 EU member states of 22 percent, while the Polish report predicted that electricity prices in Poland would increase by 60 percent. Through this move, the European Commission constructed a European scale for trading European carbon dioxide emissions. As this chapter will present, that scale and that object – European carbon dioxide emissions – were carefully and gradually deconstructed by Polish actors and those with whom they were allied.

Until July 2008, the position of the Polish government was to ask for an opt-out for Polish electricity-producing companies from auctions of EUAs. They demanded that Polish utility companies continue to be allowed to emit carbon dioxide free of charge. However, this demand

Table 2.1 Differences between the Commission's and EnergSys's assessments of the new ETS Directive's impact on the European and Polish economy

	Commission analysis	*EnergSys analysis*
Increase in power generation costs by 2020	In EU-27 by 23–33%	In Poland by 65–80%
Increase in electricity prices by 2020	In EU-27 by 19–26%	In Poland by 60%
Increase in power consumption costs for households by 2020	In EU-27 by 4.4–6.8%	In Poland by 19%
Proportion of energy consumption costs in household budgets by 2020	In EU-27 by 10%	In Poland by 16%

Source: Jankowski (2008).

Note: EU-27 refers to all EU member states between 2007 and 2013.

was not easy to justify. How would Polish carbon dioxide be different from other types of carbon dioxide emitted in the EU? Various self-Orientalizing discourses were used by Polish politicians and Green Effort Group (GEG) lobbyists. The first article produced with a GEG lobbyist's input was published in the *European Voice* newspaper in mid-2008, titled "A breakthrough or a breakdown" (Żmijewski 2008). The article outlined the dangers posed by the new ETS to the Polish economy. According to a Polish expert, existing economic inequalities would be perpetuated if industries and power sector companies from across the EU were forced to purchase emission allowances on a common market. Smaller companies with less capital, such as Polish power sector companies, would have to bid against bigger rivals in pan-European auctions. The bigger and richer companies, such as E.ON, RWE and EDF, would be able to invest more capital into buying up larger volumes of emission allowances (EUAs) while they were still relatively cheap, and then sell them when demand increased and they became more expensive. This was the first argument made against full auctions for Polish power sector companies and for a larger emission cap for Poland: unfair competition from foreign capital. The article showed that energy politics were still largely analysed in national terms, and that the largest corporations were imagined as productive forces for national economies. In 2008, a new country-specific policy nexus for climate change and energy security (see Kuzemko 2013) was established in Poland. This perspective was also underpinned by the legalistic argument that according to the Maastricht Treaty on European Union, determination of a country's energy mix lay within the national government's competence.

In July 2008, another article concerning Poland's situation in regard to new EU ETS was published in the German newspaper *Die Zeit*. The article was called "The Anxiety of Pygmies" (Tenbrock and Tatje 2008) and the headline read: "Europe is fighting for climate protection. The Continent is threatened with rupture as the East is anxious about its economic growth." The article was based on an interview with Krzysztof Żmijewski who ended it by "drawing three large figures on a piece of paper, like from a cartoon, next to which he drew three smaller ones. 'The big ones are the Maasai, the small ones are the Pygmies', says Żmiejewski and asks, 'how will the race between them end?'" He continues: "The Pygmies are not able to catch up with the Maasai, the East is not able to keep up with the West, and Poland is not able to keep up with Germany." This imaginative rhetorical trick introduced a clear division between "the big West" and "the small East". It also gave little hope for the future, since the Pygmies' short legs would never let them catch up with the long-legged Maasai (Tenbrock and Tatje 2008). In the *Die Zeit* article, Żmijewski tried to emphasize the differences between the developed West and the developing East, and to introduce an image to depict the different productive potentials of the two European regions. The Polish energy expert essentialized this difference through the biological metaphor of short-legged Pygmies and long-legged Maasais to show the close relation between carbon dioxide politics and biopolitics.

In the *Die Zeit* article (Żmijewsiki 2008) and in the Polish media, Żmijewski pointed out the significance of the emission reductions in CEE countries in the early 1990s. He pointed out that in 2004 emissions in the new member states were 23 percent lower than in 1990. The Czech Republic had reduced its emissions by around 20 percent, Poland by around 27 percent and Slovakia by 25 percent. He argued that these earlier reduction efforts should be taken into account in the ETS today and in the future. One way of doing so would be to shift the base year for 2013–2020 emission reductions from 2005 – the year proposed by the Commission in 2008 – to 1990 – the year before the post-Communist economic meltdown (Tenbrock and Tatje 2008). This idea has also been strongly promoted by the Polish mining and energy trade unions. The leader of the Secretariat of Mining and Energy Workers' Solidarność union argued for this shift during our conversation in October 2008:

> Every country should be treated individually in regard to carbon emission reductions, especially since Poland signed the Kyoto Protocol, and by the time it joined the European Union, it managed to reduce emissions by 500 percent of what it declared. And now I ask: so what? Having joined the EU, which did not meet its Kyoto reduction targets, we are now forced to help the EU make up for its failure. The EU failed, while we reduced over 500 percent of what we were supposed to have reduced and now we have to make the same reduction effort once again.
>
> (Interview 1)

However, from Brussels' point of view, free allocation of EUAs meant granting Poland free carbon dioxide emissions, which seemed a very controversial idea. At the time, the EU was taking a sharp turn towards global climate action leadership. Having realized that goal, the lobbying strategy of the GEG changed and different Polish actors strived to scale up the Polish problem with the ETS into a European problem, and thus to Europeanize Polish carbon dioxide emissions and look for other actors who also wanted to maintain the right to emit carbon dioxide for free. The consequent Europeanization of Polish carbon dioxide emissions occurred through a number of different actors assembled into different configurations within Polish and non-Polish networks. For example, although it was the Polish government's idea to ask for opt-outs from full auctioning for existing power plants in Poland, it was a group of German MEPs cooperating with German power sector companies who transformed this solution and asked for an extension of the free allocations to also include coal-fired power plants built in Poland in the future. German power sector lobbyists wanted to make sure that if they invested in Poland their future carbon dioxide emissions would not cost them a penny. A Finnish MEP and Vice President of the Committee on the Environment, Public Health and Food Safety pointed this out to me during an interview:

> Quite late in the process the Polish proposal for derogation for the existing power plants turned into a proposal for derogation also for new coal-fired power stations. And we've heard from German MEPs that this idea actually came from RWE and some other German power companies. This was lobbied for by Poland but came from Germany. We've heard from Germans that this formulation first appeared in a text by RWE because RWE and some other German power companies wanted to invest in Poland in new coal-fired power stations, and then they convinced the Poles to demand this also but that was defeated during the December Summit. ... Maybe for the Polish people it's interesting to know that there was not only a Polish interest, but also a German power sector interest to demand these derogations – the interest of the future investors.
>
> (Interview 2)

The proposal for free carbon dioxide emissions for electricity producers remained on the Polish negotiation agenda until the end of 2008, but since mid-2008 another proposal had begun to taken shape. This was a method for allocating emission allowances (EUAs) based on technological benchmarks with an ex post adjustment. This quite complicated algorithm was designed by and lobbied for by European industries – the European arm of the International Federation of Industrial Energy Consumers (IFIEC Europe) – and it was positively reviewed by an important consulting company, EcoFys (Interview 3). In July 2008 an expert from the Polish energy think tank EnergSys presented the Office for the European Integration Committee (UKIE) with a strong recommendation to support the IFIEC method and to include it in the Polish negotiating position. The same recommendation came to the Polish Ministry of the Environment from a German affiliate of the IFIEC,

Verband der Industriellen Energie- und Kraftwirtschaft (VIK), even earlier in February 2008. However, as one governmental official later told me, at that time the Ministry of the Environment did not find the VIK's presentation of the IFIEC method relevant. Polish Ministry officials and experts did not understand how that proposal would be able to save electricity producers' money or help the Polish economy. Regardless, the EnergSys expert, who was also present at the February meeting, contacted the IFIEC himself. In July, together with GEG lobbyists, he managed to persuade a high-level official in the UKIE that the IFIEC method was beneficial for Polish power companies and industries, explaining that it would reduce the cost of carbon dioxide emissions. The Polish Ministry decided to give it a try and telephoned the IFIEC Europe personally. During an interview with me, the EnergSys expert explained:

> I tried to point out that the Ministry's proposal to postpone full auctions for the Polish power sector was not a good one. Different countries are in different situations and this proposal makes it difficult to come up with general arguments that would have a Europe-wide reach. This was not a proposal that could be beneficial for a larger group of countries. After the VIK's presentation I suggested not sticking to the proposal for derogation for the Polish power sector but to emphasize that Poland wanted a solution that would have less impact on the level of electricity prices and thus show that Poland was open to alternative allocation methodologies – just like the one worked out by the IFIEC.
>
> (Interview 4)

The IFIEC method, in the eyes of its own designers, was above all a project for lowering electricity prices in Europe. And low electricity prices were not only vital for households but also for industries. As the UKIE official told me, the interest of "the Polish economy" was to keep Polish industries globally competitive, and thus to supply them with cheap labour and electricity. In order to grasp this challenge, European industries coined the concept "carbon leakage". This evoked an image of carbon dioxide emissions escaping the economic and political area of the EU, where they were priced high, and sneaking into other areas around the world where they did not even have a price. The concept of "carbon dioxide leakage" also evoked images of other types of leakage, such as the outflow of jobs, capital and growth to other regions. Therefore, these different designs for the ETS co-produced (Jasanoff 2004) different categories of carbon dioxide: free and priced carbon dioxide, Polish carbon dioxide, European carbon dioxide, future carbon dioxide from German investments in Poland, carbon dioxide fleeing outside of Europe together with European growth, etc. All of these categories were highly political and implied different visions for development, different futures and differently scaled EU member states as spaces for development.

The boundaries of the Polish lobbying network were shifting. Different categories of carbon dioxide were used to bound new actors (carbon dioxide emissions could also be conceptualized as a boundary object after Griesemer and Star (1989)) and mobilize them around a particular policy proposal. Thanks to the IFIEC method, Polish actors could finally move away from their self-Orientalizing strategy. They had a piece of solid Western expertise reviewed by the renowned Western consulting company EcoFys and could start enrolling more actors from Central Eastern Europe, not by referring to their common historical experience of a traumatic post-socialist transformation but rather by bringing up the technological commonalities among them.

Carbon dioxide emissions from Polish Coal and Russian Gas

Although the Polish government and Polish power sector companies and industries in general accepted the IFIEC method, the method did not exactly match the Polish project for low electricity prices. The type of fuel mattered. According to my interviewee from the Ministry of Economy, the IFIEC method was not particularly good for Poland because it defined the allocation of free allowances based on a general benchmark for the electricity sector. The amount of free allowances would be set according to the least carbon dioxide-intensive fossil fuel-based technologies in the power sector – and this meant technologies using natural gas. For Polish governmental actors, on the other hand, it meant that "Polish coal" would lose out to "Russian gas" because the latter emitted less carbon dioxide per 1 MWh of produced electricity. Almost 50 percent less carbon dioxide is emitted when 1 MWh of electricity is produced from natural gas (514.85 kg/MWh) as compared to coal (1020 kg/MWh). High efficiency natural gas-fired power stations can produce up to 70 percent fewer greenhouse gas emissions than existing brown coal-fired generators. The Polish actors understood this as favouring gas over coal. Therefore, the Polish government, together with the UKIE official and the EnergSys expert, modified the original IFIEC method and proposed a fuel-specific benchmark for power sector companies (Interview 5) to their Brussels colleagues. This meant that there would be different rules for gas and for coal for allocating free allowances to emit carbon dioxide. Coal would not compete against gas; rather power sector companies would be evaluated separately with regard to their emission intensity. Carbon dioxide emitted from coal would thus constitute a different category of carbon dioxide to be governed, priced and reduced than carbon dioxide from natural gas. The main expert from the IFIEC commented on this innovation as follows:

> We had a long debate about it. Germans are also more or less on the fuel-specific side. But the Ecofys report clearly says that if you want to go to low carbon technology, then you must not have a fuel-specific benchmark because then you simply go on building coal-fired power plants.
>
> (Interview 6)

The IFIEC expert recommended to Poles yet another idea – to go for regionally differentiated benchmarks. He proposed distinguishing three or five areas wherein emissions trading would take place. One area would be CEE, with its large dominance of coal in electricity production and a higher benchmark. Another trading region with a separate benchmark would consist of Germany and Benelux, while the UK could also have its own benchmark (Interview 6). This was yet another idea for how the controversial object – carbon dioxide – could be classified and differentiated according to different regions in Europe. However, with the highest share of coal in electricity production, Poland was not happy to be packed together with other CEE countries that have nuclear power plants and a lot of hydropower installations. Poles still preferred the fuel-specific benchmark. "We have no Alps!" exclaimed Żmijewski at the hearing in the House of Lords in October 2008, to explain why Poland does not have hydropower plants. Poland has an abundance of coal, argued Jerzy Buzek at the same meeting:

> Lord Palmer: Is all the coal that you burn home produced?
> Professor Buzek: Yes, 100%. We are also selling some coal. It depends on the year and on the activity of our coal mining industry 10%/5% and it was always the same a few years ago, 20 years ago and 30 years ago ... From the point of view of production, about 100 million tonnes per year, 95——99 million tonnes per year. We had a big amount of lignite, first of all, and we did not use it until now at all, so we are waiting for the start, if it will be possible. For hard coal we also have a big amount today, for 30 or 40 years at least, and if we start to explore quite new parts of our country, it could be even for 100 or 120 years. Underground gasification could

bring it even for 300 years, because its depth is about 1,200–1,500 meters below the sea level. Then, if we develop underground gasification, it would be for 300 years, because there is an enormous amount of coal on this level.

(House of Lords 2008)

Coal was framed as a domestic fuel in this debate, even though a lot of that resource was being imported, including from Russia. Buzek concluded this part of the discussion in the House of Lords quite abruptly: "Our political independence means nuclear, coal and the renewables" (House of Lords 2008). Why would only these three types of fuels be politically acceptable in Poland? Why was natural gas excluded from this list? The answer to this question was given many times by Polish actors during the hearing in the House of Lords, at meetings with representatives of the Commission and in the press. In a *Die Zeit* article from July 2008 (Tenbrock and Tatje 2008), the GEG lobbyist pointed out that there was a fear shared by Poland and other Eastern European states that "switching from coal to gas" would push them into new (old) political dependencies. Russia's Gazprom could increase its influence in the region. An official from the Czech Republic quoted in *Die Zeit* stated: "Of course, we could replace coal with a less polluting fuel such as Russian natural gas, but the question is whether we want to reduce emission by becoming more dependent on Russia?" (Tenbrock and Tatje 2008). The GEG lobbyist, in his correspondence with the Commission official Matthias Reute, also referred to this issue:

> I understand that the main goal of the 3x20 program is to guarantee emission reductions by 20 percent till 2020 … and not to "switch to less emitting fossil fuels" (in other words, natural gas), which you have stated in your letter. According to the declaration of Member States, the latter can be treated only as an emission reduction tool – a tool among many other tools, such as energy efficiency, development of renewable resources, carbon capture and storage and nuclear energy. I am deeply concerned that treating the goal of "switching from coal to gas" as the main one pushes Poland and other countries – for example Baltic states – straight into the claws of Gazprom.
>
> (Żmijewski 2008)

A fuel-specific benchmark would therefore allow for the separate treatment of coal and gas because of their distinct "geopolitical values". These two resources were an integral part of geopolitics, and each carried a completely different meaning for energy security and political autonomy in the CEE region. The Greenpeace report (2008) on the dirtiest fossil fuel – coal – did not account for these political factors. For representatives of the CEE states, it was not simply a question of burning 1 kg of coal and 1 kg of natural gas and measuring their carbon dioxide emissions. That was an overly simplistic approach – for the Polish actors especially. In Poland, establishing equivalence between coal and natural gas involved considerations about economic and political independence from its great Eastern neighbour. These two resources were not politically neutral, nor was the carbon dioxide emitted from burning each of them. The issue of the security of energy supplies was not a trivial one, and Poland together with six other new EU member states – all former Communist states – asked for "the security of energy supplies to be included in the bloc's planned climate strategy". Fear of Russia has long been deeply embedded in the social imagination in the CEE region (Zarycki 2004). "Political fossil fuels" could thus become the basis for new divisions in the EU.

Carbon dioxide, capital and the Polish state

Poland's objections to full auctions for power sector companies were condemned by the European environmental movement. The biggest environmental NGOs with offices in Brussels, including the World Wide Fund for Nature (WWF), Greenpeace, Oxfam and Friends of the Earth, as well as environmental umbrella organizations such the Climate Action Network Europe (CAN Europe) and the European Environmental Bureau, were against any free allocation of emission allowances to power sector companies. CAN Europe's officials were proud to tell me during an interview that their biggest moral success within the last two years was to teach the public that windfall profits for power producers were geared by free allocation of emission allowances and that they were immoral. In other words, carbon dioxide emissions that were free of charge were immoral. Therefore, they welcomed and endorsed the Commission's proposal for full auctions for the power sector, where every tonne of carbon dioxide emitted would need to be paid for by companies. Brussels-based NGOs perceived the strategy of the Polish government as being manipulated by power producers not only in Poland, but also German and Swedish companies such as RWE, Vattenfall and E.ON. In a report published jointly by CAN Europe, Friends of the Earth Europe, WWF and Greenpeace (2008), NGOs accused the Polish government of seeking to undermine the European

Climate Change and Energy Package. In the introduction to the report they pointed out:

> This briefing, based on independent economic analysis, explains how the proposal by the Polish government to continue the free allocation of pollution permits to the electricity sector will not reduce power prices and overall energy costs for Polish families and businesses. The briefing shows how free allocation could mean transferring significant amounts of money out of Poland to shareholders of utility companies, such as RWE, Vattenfall and E.ON. This will happen at the expense of labour tax relief, energy efficiency programmes or other measures that can help Polish families and businesses to reduce their energy costs.
>
> (CAN Europe et al. 2008, p. 1)

In the report, the NGOs touched upon issues sensitive for the Polish public and the government, namely the issue of power sector privatization:

> The Polish electricity sector is the largest in Central and Eastern Europe. The Polish coal and associated power-generation industry are in the process of major restructuring, because of market liberalization and the prospect of old plants being retired. It's not a surprise that European utility giants, such as RWE, Vattenfall and E.ON, as well as suppliers of power plant equipment, see the current Polish market situation as an opportunity for growth ... the major European utility companies have ambitions to increase their activities in the Polish power sector by both investing in new generation capacity and through merger and acquisition activities.
>
> (CAN Europe et al. 2008, p. 2)

Furthermore, they pointed out that Polish utility companies lacked capital for the substantial investments that were necessary to keep the Polish power sector on track (CAN Europe et al. 2008, pp. 2–3). According to the report, with European utility giants acquiring a larger market share in the Polish power sector, their windfall profits could end up in the pockets of the shareholders of RWE, Vattenfall and E.ON (CAN Europe et al. 2008, p. 3). According to their calculations, the proposal for full auctions would generate approximately 2–9 billion euros in revenue for the Polish budget.

While green NGOs saw an opposition between keeping revenues in the state budgets and keeping them in companies' pockets, Polish experts and Polish government officials alike argued that this opposition was wrong. The IFIEC method, which they supported, would indeed reduce revenues for state budgets, but it would not increase revenues for the power sector companies. It would only make the cost of the emissions trade lower. The GEG lobbyist (Żmijewski 2008) pointed to the "real" reasons why the Commission was against the IFIEC method: it did "not generate the super-high prices [sic] needed to promote new, economically non-viable technologies" and it did "not generate high income which could be spent by the Commission and States outside of the EU". In this way he accused the Commission of showing "an impatient drive for developing new technologies and carrying out big civilizing projects" Once again the language of ordering, developing, modernizing and civilizing was brought into the debate, this time as an accusation against the Commission's political ideas. He pointed out that these motivations would "not necessarily be endorsed by EU citizens, especially those working their way up" (Żmijewski 2008). With these statements, the GEG lobbyist showed that Poland was not ready to jump on the bandwagon of technological and economic progress. Poland was still "working its way up", it was still involved in an old project for development – a carbon dioxide intensive one that Orientalized it as a new EU member state and an economy in transition.

This part of the debate also points to a different conception for the state and the state's role with regard to capital and its citizens. While the European green movement saw it as natural that governments would like to gain a bigger share of revenues from emissions trading, the Polish government decided to fight for lower electricity prices in Poland at the cost of gaining less revenue from emissions trading. While the European environmental movement wished to see governments organizing and funding climate policy measures and having control over re-distribution of emissions trade revenues, the Polish government tried to maintain the competitive advantage of the Polish economy as an economy with cheap electricity. The Polish government therefore defined its role as mainly that of a guarantor of national economic competitiveness. In the debate on carbon dioxide emission reductions, the Polish state's role was framed by governmental actors as that of an industrial "competition state" (see Fougner 2006). Poland was competing with other states for investments, trying to keep industrial companies within its borders and to attract more capital for the future. Here Poland was a neo-liberal state assuming the role of an organizer of favourable conditions for capital to extract value within the state's boundaries (see Brown 2003).

EU Summits, carbon dioxide and a European scale for climate action

In the final phase of negotiations, Poland pushed through the fuel-specific benchmark allocation of three emission allowances as a solution that could be applied to countries covered by the derogation period between 2013 and the end of 2019 (Interview 5). The final victories of the Polish negotiation team during the December meeting were:

- a gradual inclusion of the Polish power sector into the system of full carbon dioxide emission allowance auctions within the EU ETS (70 percent of free emission allowances in 2013)
- exclusion of free emission allowances for the Polish power sector from the EU ETS
- a revision clause offering the possibility to prolong free emission allocations for the Polish power sector in 2018
- a larger share of the EU carbon dioxide emission allowances for Poland
- flexibility in choosing the base year for emission reduction (emissions from 2005 or average emissions from the period 2005–2007).

The negotiation outcome was framed by Polish actors as a success – as Poland's success in the EU. However, derogations meant that the logic of exceptions had won, and the solutions supported and proposed by the Polish actors were not upscaled to become EU-abiding rules. The amendment that was added showed that EU member states could not all work towards carbon dioxide emission reduction at the same pace, and that some countries needed more time to prepare or they might never be able to catch up. In the media, the East–West divide was the dominant frame for presenting diverging ideas for how the European carbon trade could be organized. In October 2008, the international media reported that Poland along with other new member states (Hungary, the Czech Republic, Slovakia, Lithuania, Latvia, Estonia, Bulgaria and Romania) obstructed the decision-making process at the European Council Summit of 15–16 October 2008 and forced the postponement of a final decision on the Climate Change and Energy Package until the December Summit, where it would be adopted unanimously. But if one takes a closer look at the negotiation process, the division of interests ran along lines that did not necessarily coincide with a division between the new post-socialist member states and the old liberal market economies in Western Europe. Rather, the division of interests ran according to the composition of energy mixes in the electricity-producing sectors and along different sectors of industrial production. Thus, the problem of constructing a European scale for emission reduction policies cannot be understood through a simple East–West lens. It shows once again the effect that fuels and technologies have on economic and political systems (Mitchell 2011). One of my interviewees from CAN Europe drew such a picture of the October Summit:

> You had many Central and Eastern European member states who were upset with the 2005 baseline ... You also had the power sector with full auctioning which was the main issue in the Baltic States, Poland and the Czech Republic, and then you had Germany coming in, which had an issue with auctioning for the industry as a whole and also with regard to auctioning for the power sector more and less, but they were then again pushed by RWE for getting that out there and those companies, on their own terms, were lobbying CEE governments. They were playing a very dirty game and that created in October 2008, right after the vote in the European Parliament, this tremendous uprising at the first State Head and government meeting, where Sarkozy was faced with an opposition he didn't expect. And he said, ok we can deal with some CEE MSs where, he said, we would buy them at a certain point with more revenues, but then he had Italy joining and he had Germany acting and that was not solvable. So what he did in the end was to say ok, we see there is a problem, I'm going to take it in my hands. The Environment Council and also the Parliament were not really going to look at them but if there is a deal it will be done at Heads of State and Government level and also it will be done by unanimity – all big decisions are going to be taken by unanimity.
>
> (Interview 7)

Interestingly, the CAN Europe expert pointed out that the French President, Nicolas Sarkozy, wanted to buy those CEE states with more state budget revenue and that this easy solution would not work with the old member states. Did they not need more budget revenues? Was there some other logic for persuading Western states to accept the proposal made by the European Commission? So far, analysis has shown that the East–West divide (Melegh 2005; Zarycki 2004) with Orientalizing discourses has been constructed mainly by actors coming from CEE member states such as Poland. This excerpt shows that the East–West construction has also been made by the Western actors. The East represented the needy part of Europe, which could be easily satisfied with some "development money". The West represented the developed part of Europe, which could not be simply bought by offered money. A Polish governmental official whom I interviewed also commented on the impact of the new member states on the decisions made during the October Summit as follows:

> We have not officially raised this issue but in the then binding Treaty in article 175, paragraph 1c or 2c there is a line that legal initiatives significantly changing the structure of member states' energy mixes should be made unanimously. We even had some legal expertise with us, but we were not telling the Commission that they were doing it against the law or that they were trying to push the decision on the Package through in the co-decision procedure. We framed our arguments in a political way saying that this legal act was of great importance. We were saying that it is strategic for the power sector, for the economies, for the future position of the European economies globally. And at this point there was a really strong coalition of countries, not only the new member states but also the Italians and, surprisingly, even the Germans were afraid that a decision made during the October Summit would not be good for them. The Germans were mainly afraid of carbon leakage. And Sarkozy's ambition to have the Package adopted by the end of his Presidency was also an important factor. When he encountered opposition towards the co-decision procedure in October he then decided the final vote would be cast during the meeting of the European Council in December.
>
> (Interview 5)

The October decision to postpone the final vote on the Package of directives until the December Council meeting was an important moment in the negotiations. According to my interviewee from the Polish government's UKIE office, this improved the negotiating position of Poland. This was due to simple arithmetic. Before the October decision, the proposed directives (among them the EU's ETS Directive) would be voted on by a qualified majority procedure. Poland had only 27 votes. The blocking minority was 94 votes. Until mid-October the absolutely key question addressed to Poland was "Have you already built a qualified majority to block the Package?" After the October Summit the question was, "Are you satisfied with the Package?" The governmental official told me that "this fundamentally changed the character of our work – of the negotiation process" (Interview3).

After the October meeting, the Polish Ministry of Economy set out to look for more allies and to build a stronger coalition of countries. An official from the Ministry told me that based on an analysis the government had conducted about the impact of auctions on electricity prices, they had managed to persuade the Italians, Bulgarians, Romanians, Hungarians and the Baltic states that they would face similar problems as Poland. They also organized meetings with business representatives from these countries. They met with MEPs, while the Polish government contacted other governments, trying to make them act by saying, "Look, what are you waiting for? You are a Chamber of Commerce, you are a business council so move on and go talk to your Ministers, go and talk to your Prime Minister, to your President, to your Ambassadors and tell them what the situation looks like" (Interview 4).

However, the coalition was in fact much weaker than it seemed after a series of more or less formal meetings, and the shape of the ETS Directive and of other legislative proposals of the Package remained in question until the last moment of the negotiations. The December Summit was the arena where the final decision was to be taken. The UKIE official told me that the final decisions were made in the lobbies of the December Summit. The Polish negotiation team tried to "smash this Summit several times ... once on Thursday and once on Friday" (Interview3). He told me, "We were simply saying: these are our conditions for taking a unanimous decision. And we were saying in a straightforward manner that the proposals of the French Presidency did not fulfill our expectations" (Interview 3).

Despite this attitude, the reality looked more mundane. An official from the Ministry of Economy told me that in the end Poland managed to persuade some countries that the benchmark proposal was a good one. The coalition, described in the international press as "the coalition of the unwilling", was much weaker than the one presented in the media. Openly, in the December negotiation process in Poland was supported by the Lithuanian Energy Minister and by a Bulgarian Minister. A wide number of countries were opting for a gradual introduction of full auctions. And there was a large group of countries against full auctions. However, there was a divide within this group. And then, as my interviewee from the Ministry of Economy told me:

> We came up with the proposal for fuel-specific benchmarks and gained the support of a couple of countries. The rest were saying: ok but we don't think this can go through, thus, it's better that we hold on to the gradual introduction of full auctions. And in fact, in December we were sitting down to the negotiation table quite lonely as to the alternative benchmark proposal. Maybe it was not even such a bad thing to make an impression on those observing

the negotiations that there was a strong coalition, but such a strong coalition did not in fact exist.

(Interview 5)

While Poland sought to enrol other member states into its project for fuel-specific benchmarks, the French Presidency was proceeding with its counter-enrolment activities:

> The French Presidency was lobbying intensively for full auctions. Their main argument was that there would be huge revenues from auctions and that this money could be spent by governments on modernization of their grid and power sector infrastructure. They promised the Estonians, for example, easier access to public funds. Therefore, most of the countries, while sitting down at the negotiation table were ready to accept full auctions – except for Poland. And thanks to the decisions made during the October Summit, where with considerable input from our negotiators we managed to change the decision-making procedure for the Package from a co-decision to a unanimous decision at the European Council. There we had the advantage of not being in a completely lost position, and we managed to get this derogation in the end. As we learned later from the Czechs, Slovaks, Bulgarians and Romanians, they were all going to use the right for opt-outs from full auctions. But this was not a strong coalition.
>
> (Interview 5)

In December again, as during the October Summit, it mattered whether the opposition came from new or old member states:

> There is such a rule in the EU that if you want to make a deal, you have to have at least one big country from the old member states on your side. Then you may have a chance to win something over. Our coalition was a coalition made of new, let's say, weak member states – states that were easy to influence … and thanks to the various manoeuvres of the Commission and of the French Presidency they sat down at the negotiation table "pacified" … well, right, the Hungarians were still raising their voices and arguing for taking into account the reduction effort made under the Kyoto Protocol. So Poland and Hungary, these were the only two countries fighting for their interests openly. The rest were completely "pacified".
>
> (Interview 5)

Italy, an alleged ally of the new member states, was in fact not pursuing the same goals as the benchmark coalition:

> The Italians made a lot of noise but in fact they only cared about the Cars Directive. The media was reporting that the Italians would block the Package, but once the Cars Directive was finalized in line with their interests, they didn't care about anything else.
>
> (Interview 5)

Interestingly, while RWE and other German companies were in favour of extending the derogation for the power sector to coal-fuelled power plants built in the future, during the December Summit the German governmental representation was very much against it. It opposed extending derogation beyond the already existing power plants. Therefore, in the last moments of the negotiations, Poland proposed extending the derogation to power plants in which the investment process had already been physically initiated:

> An investment physically initiated by the end of December 2008 was a Polish idea. We wrote it into the ETS Directive. Some half an hour before adopting the final conclusions of the European Council the Directive was saying that only existing power plants would receive free allowances. So in fact, if we closed half of our existing power plants by 2013 or 2014, well at least some 10–20 thousand MW, then we would be in a situation where the derogation covered only a very limited number of our power plants. On the other hand, the Germans were pressing hard to cover only existing power plants with this derogation, so it was difficult to prolong it beyond 2008. That's how we came up with the concept of a physically initiated investment in order to extend the derogation also to initiated power plant projects. This was a considerable success because there was a huge pressure from the Commission and Germany to prevent any kind of extension of this derogation.
>
> (Interview 5)

Conclusions

The ETS negotiations showed how difficult it can be to construct a European scale of action. However, it also showed that within the European structures of governance, the state's capacity to produce expertise and define its economic and political interests are distributed across a network of actors who span national borders. The Polish state actors enhanced their understanding of the ETS reform and the future position of Polish power sector companies and of industries operating in Poland once they engaged in conversations with experts from various industry associations and state officials from other EU member states. The Polish negotiating position was an amalgamation of ideas coming from German power sector corporations, German industry associations, European industry associations and other CEE governments – all filtered through the interest of Poland's coal-based electricity-producing sector and a fear of Russian gas suppliers.

This story has thus been analysed from two angles. First, it was shown that several political scalar effects (Simons et al. 2014) of various spaces of governance were co-produced (Jasanoff 2004) through these different processes of expertise production and the negotiation of it: the nation state, the CEE region, Eastern and Western Europe, and the EU as an integrated space of governance. Moreover, a new object was co-produced which also turned out to be politically and economically scalable – carbon dioxide emissions. Depending on the policy proposal, carbon dioxide was objectified in relation to different actors (power companies), spaces (various regions of Europe), fossil fuels (coal and gas) and geopolitics (Russia or Western Europe). It was objectified as an object with a socialist legacy, as an object of traumatic post-socialist transition and as an object involved in modernization and economic development, and each objectification was conducive to a different scale of political action, to different politics. Moreover, this chapter shows that in this debate the Polish state was co-produced in its relations with Western power producers and Western industries as a neo-liberal state (Fougner 2006) ready to make favourable conditions for foreign capital to arrive.

References

Brown, W. (2003) Neo-liberalism and the end of liberal democracy. *Theory and Event* 7(1): 1–19.

Callon, M. and Muniesa, F. (2005) Economic markets as calculative collective devices. *Organizational Studies* 26(8): 1229–1250.

Fougner, T. (2006) The state, international competitiveness and neoliberal globalization: is there a future beyond 'the competition state'? *Review of International Studies* 32: 165–185.

Griesemer, J. R. and Star, S. L. (1989) Institutional ecology, 'translations' and boundary objects: amateurs and professionals in Berkeley's Museum of Vertebrate Zoology, 1907–39. *Social Studies of Science* 19(3): 387–420.

Jasanoff, S. (ed) (2004) *States of Knowledge: The Co-Production of Science and Social Order*. New York: Routledge.

Kuzemko, C. (2013) *The Energy Security–Climate Nexus: Institutional Change in the UK and Beyond*. London: Palgrave Macmillan.
Melegh, A. (2005) *On the East–West Slope*. Budapest: CEU Press.
Mitchell, T. (2011) *Carbon Democracy: Political Power in the Age of Oil*. New York: Verso.
Simons, A., Lis, A. and Lippert, I. (2014) The political duality of scale-making in environmental markets. *Environmental Politics* 23(4): 632–649.
Zarycki, T. (2004) Uses of Russia: the role of Russia in the modern Polish national identity. *East European Politics & Societies* 18(4): 595–627.

Documents

CAN Europe, Friends of the Earth Europe, WWF and Greenpeace (2008) Free pollution permits for the Polish power sector? How Polish households are filling the pockets of European energy giants. Retrieved 15 January 2018 from http://awsassets.panda.org/downloads/0811br_poland_and_allocation_of_permits.pdf
Directive 2003/87/EC of the European Parliament and of the Council of October 2003 establishing a scheme for greenhouse gas emission allowance trading within the Community and amending Council Directive 96/61/EC, *Official Journal of the European Union*, 25 October 2003.
EnergSys (2008) Report 2030: impact of the European Commission's Energy and Climate Package of 23 January 2008 on energy system, economy and households in Poland. Warsaw: PKEE/EnergSys.
European Commission (2001) Proposal for a Directive of the European Parliament and of the Council establishing a scheme for greenhouse gas emission allowance trading within the Community and amending Council Directive 96/61/EC. COM(2001)581 final. Brussels, 23 October 2001.
European Commission (2008) Impact Assessment: Document accompanying the Package of Implementation measures for the EU's objectives on climate change and renewable energy for 2020. SEC(2008)52. Brussels, 23 January 2008.
House of Lords (2008) European Union Committee: 33rd Report of Session 2007–08: The Revision of the EU's Emission's Trading System: Report with Evidence. London: The Stationary Office Limited, HL paper 197.
Jankowski, B. (2008) *Pakiet energetyczno klimatyczny porażką czy zwycięstwem PolIki i Unii? [Climate and energy package: Poland's and the EU's success or failure?]*. Warsaw: Badania Systemowe EnergSys Sp. z o.o. Retrieved 15 May 2019 from www.energsys.com.pl/fileadmin/pdf/03_Ekspertyza_Pakiet.pdf

Media reports

Tenbrock, C. and Tatje, C. (2008) Die Angst der Pygmäen, *Die Zeit* (10 July 2008). Retrieved 9 December 2009 from www.zeit.de/2008/29/Klima-Osteuropa

Żmijewski, K. (2008) Breakthrough or breakdown? *EuropeanVoice.com* (4 July 2008).

Interviews

Interview 1: Leader of the Secretariat of Mining and Energy Workers' union Solidarność, Warsaw, October 2008.
Interview 2: Finish MEP, Rapporteur of the Effort Sharing Directive, Brussels, April 2009.
Interview 3: Expert at FEWE, Warsaw, January 2009.
Interview 4: UKIE official, Warsaw, February 2009.
Interview 5: DG Environment, Director, Brussels, July 2009.
Interview 6: Expert at IFIEC, Brussels, June 2009.
Interview 7: Negotiator of the ETS Directive, Permanent Representation of the Republic of Poland, Brussels, March 2009.

3 Production of expertise, scaling and shale gas in Poland

Introduction

In this chapter, I argue that shale gas in Poland constitutes a particularly important energy object, valued mainly as a strategic resource for the economy and Poland's energy security. In 2011, the US Energy Information Agency (EIA 2011) published an assessment of natural gas and oil resources in shale rock formations worldwide. According to the report, Poland had the second largest reserve of all European countries, second only to France. With these numbers, shale gas entered energy politics in Poland as a potentially highly valuable resource. However, given its materiality – shale gas being trapped over three thousand metres below the surface – a great deal of capital and expertise had to be invested in its transformation into a resource, which in the end failed. Moreover, through EU membership, shale gas was contextualized by the energy security–climate change nexus and other environmental concerns. EU institutions played an important role in bringing these extra-economic and extra-security valuations of shale gas to the forefront. A short history of shale gas exploration in Poland – a couple of years of debates and subsoil activities – placed Poland in the new context of resource politics, which was mainly played out between the US, the EU and – indirectly, in a sometimes imaginary way – Russia.

Expertise on shale gas was produced by two types of actors: economic experts and geologists. While the former, usually based in think tanks or consulting companies, produced various assessments of the profitability of shale gas extraction, the latter produced knowledge about accessible volumes and the environmental impacts of extraction technologies. These different types of expertise, however, all hinged upon the ability to operate underground, to explore the subsoil physically and learn about its structure and composition. In this chapter, I argue that an interesting dependency was created: all knowledge-producing actors depended on capital investment into resource exploration, without which there would be no data to operate on, with which to make plans or predictions about the economic and environmental future of the project. In other words, global capital was an important part of the co-production of the different kinds of expertise about the resource and the resource itself.

While most of these operations were carried out in Poland, an interesting situation emerged. The data analysing the rock formations and the shale gas resource, as well as the environmental impacts of hydraulic fracturing in Europe were mostly coming from Poland and, as the European Commission and other EU bodies were interested in regulating a newly emerging resource industry, they needed to rely on some of these data in order to understand potential impacts or create development scenarios. Thus, this chapter also examines the interesting interactions between Polish geologists and EU-level officials from the Joint Research Centre (JRC) working within the European Science and Technology Network on Unconventional Hydrocarbon Extraction (UH Network), which was established by the European Commission in 2015 to collect reliable information on the available technologies for the hydraulic fracturing of shale rock and their environmental impacts. Since most of the exploration activities were taking place in Poland and the Polish Geological Institute (PGI) was the only institution in Europe conducting empirical research with a baseline study on the environmental impacts of fracking in seven different locations in Poland, the Polish expertise constituted a substantial contribution to the work of the UH Network.

However, the process of making Polish expertise relevant to EU-level deliberations, of scaling it up to the EU level, was not an automatic one. This was achieved through establishing relations between Polish geologists and other EU-level actors within the institutional framework of the UH Network. It is argued in this chapter that the UH Network operated as a scaling mechanism for the expertise produced in Poland. The chapter concludes with a reflection that co-production of expertise and resources also involved negotiations and the emergence of different scales at which shale gas would function as an object: local, national, European and global. Both the negotiations and their effects should be seen as highly political endeavours.

Producing expertise on shale gas as a resource: the state–nature–capital nexus

Shale gas as a resource, as I have already pointed out, is not something that can simply be found, but it is something that needs to be constructed physically, economically, politically and ontologically (see Kama 2019). If we follow Moore (2015) in his thinking about resources, a resource appears to be an object that is co-produced by human activity in and through nature. At the same time, there is something more specific about how capitalism needs resources and how it works in and through nature in order to make and consume them. Only by becoming a resource does nature hold any value within the capitalist system. Resourceless nature is worthless for capital. Nature is cheap for the capital unless it is made into a resource or assigned other non-productive values by actors (e.g. states or civil society). Therefore, while studying how shale gas is being made into a resource, it is useful to reiterate some of Moore's (2015) questions: "How do we view nature in part or as a whole, as valuable? ... How are the valuations of nature practised – through markets, states, and ideas – in the modern world?" (p. 51). Due to the existence of these other non-business actors and their ideas about the environmental and social impacts of resource extraction, the valuation of shale gas as a resource became highly controversial and was politicized. It occurred at a time when the broader scope of nature's valuation was changing, mainly due to concerns about climate change in the era of the Anthropocene.

Therefore, following Moore (2015), I claim that the concept of "nature as matrix", within which capitalism unfolds to appropriate shale gas as a resource, has been subjected to re-configuration due to scientific and political realizations about the increasing levels of anthropogenic greenhouse gas emissions and the changing global climate. As a potent greenhouse gas, shale gas (methane) represented different values for different actors. While it was a potentially valuable resource for companies although its value depended on weighing the cost of using and developing technologies for its exploration, as well as the costs of different fees and permits, against its market value, climate and environmental protection activists opposed fracking on a number ofdifferent grounds. Most, however, were concerned about the impacts of burning yet more fossil fuels. They also opposed the "law of cheap nature" (Moore 2015, p. 53) and strove to increase the value of nature, or even exclude it from companies' operations, by lobbying for more regulations, environmental fees, bans and moratoriums, or by simply obstructing companies' activities in the field. At the same time, the state actors saw the potential for additional budget revenues from shale gas production and they worked towards making it politically valuable.

In the case of Poland, with the US EIA report (2011) at hand and the various data collected by the Polish geological institutions in the 1960s and 1970s, the Polish government issued exploration licences to around seventy companies in the early 2010s, hoping to see quick returns from shale gas as a resource. The initial strategy adopted by the Polish state was indeed that of "cheap nature". In a set of interviews carried out by Grzegorz Makuch and published in 2014 as a collection (Makuch 2014), we see, for example, how the Head of Exploration Activities at the Institute of Oil and Gas in Kraków supported a strategy to issue companies with many cheap licences for exploration activities (Makuch 2014, p. 43). His perception was that "companies were risking a lot and spending a lot of money to look for the resource" (Makuch 2014, p. 43) and therefore an ideal and desirable situation would be to provide companies with favourable conditions for the swift extraction of shale gas in the near future. The Polish state would receive high revenues from extraction fees and taxes in the production phase. Thus, the government with its licensing strategy and field of experts did not mind creating an Orientalized space for resource extraction companies, as they were counting on a share of the shale gas boom in the state budget.

However, the actual level of engagement from oil and gas companies was very low. At the beginning of 2012, 109 licences had already been given out, but only 18 wells had been fractured. Faced with this poor result, the Ministry of the Treasury hoped that Polish power-producing companies would get involved in fracking operations by investing capital into shale gas projects run by the Polish state-owned oil and gas company, PGNiG. However, according to a Polish MEP, Bogusław Sonik, it was vital for the Polish shale gas project to attract financially robust foreign companies. Drilling for shale gas was capital-intensive (Makuch 2014, p. 14–15) and the exploration phase involved learning how valuable that layer of subsoil, that piece of nature, was for different actors. And while the companies were pressing for more information about the extractable resources and state taxation rates, various actors from the EU policy arena were busy researching the environmental impacts of this new industry.

In 2011, the Polish Geological Institute (PGI) analysed archival data on shale gas resources and in 2012 published a report which included an updated assessment of the amount of extractable shale gas in Poland (PGI 2012). The figures presented in the report were much lower than those previously assessed by the US EIA by between 346 and 768 billion m^3 and this had a cooling effect on the business actors (Lis and Stankiewicz 2017). The opposition party of the time criticized the report and the timing of its publication. The former Chief Country Geologist, Mariusz-Orion Jędrysek (Makuch 2014) disapproved of the government's decision to publish the PGI's report because, he argued, the PGI did not have enough data to make any meaningful assessments.

The report was based on data from 39 boreholes from 1950 to 1990 and it did not cover all sites licensed from 2011. The description of the shale rock was poor and the report underassessed the volumes of extractable shale gas. Jędrysek compared the work done by PGI to "studying quantities of carbon dioxide in a water reservoir based on a water sample that had been stored in a bottle thirty years ago" (Makuch 2014, p. 131). Geological experts from the PGI concluded that only after 300 hydraulic fracturing operations were carried out would it be possible to fully grasp the potential scale of the shale gas industry in Poland.

In addition, it soon transpired that the technology that had been used efficiently in the US was inefficient and excessively costly when applied to the exploration shale rock in Poland.[1] In 2011, the Polish government decided to allocate billions of Polish zloty to research new fracking methods. The National Centre for Research and Development (NCBiR) together with the Agency for Industrial Development established a funding scheme called Blue Gas.[2] The scheme provided grants for the development and testing of pilot projects for new fracking technologies which could then be implemented by Polish companies, awarded in two waves between 2012 and 2013. This programme also came about as part of a response by state institutions to the growing dependence on foreign capital and technologies. Blue Gas also had the aim of experimenting with other media that could replace water in fracking operations. A new method could potentially save a lot of fresh water. However, even pilot projects rely on underground operations and these are extremely costly. A combination of state funding and capital investment was needed to developing these new technologies. The programme ends in 2022, but to date no results from the project have been released. The latest news item on the Blue Gas programme's website is dated September 2014 and lists the winners of the second round of the competition.[3]

Interdependency between state funding and capital investment in regard to generating revenue from the new resource can be observed throughout the entire short history of the shale gas project in Poland. Moore's (2015) thesis of a "double internality" of capitalism through nature and nature through capitalism cannot work without the intermediary role of the state, which can be understood as a set of institutions that prepare the state to function as a container for the capital (Foulgner 2006). This also requires making nature cheap and available for the capital, but if nature turns out to be cumbersome and less willing to cooperate cheaply with the capital, the capital may withdraw to other areas of the world. States, through their policies, can either make this double movement easier or harder by creating obstacles, introducing fees, bans and other procedures. If we look, then, at the Polish state, its role in the described process appears to be rather ambiguous. Some experts told me that the Polish government behaved as if it wanted with one hand to give things to the companies for free and with the other to take them away (Interview 1). A great deal of confusion was created by the government's proposal for new taxation schemes for the emerging industry. Not only did the proposals change numerous times within a short span of time, but the proposed numbers became higher in each round of negotiations. In 2011, the first shale gas flare was lit in Lubocino in the Pomeranian region (Górlikowski 2013). The company operating on that concession was the Polish state-owned company PGNiG, and to mark the occasion the then Prime Minister Donald Tusk came out and gave a speech about the prosperity and wealth of the country thanks to its developing shale gas industry.

In October 2012, the government proposed terms for the new law regulating taxation for the mining of hydrocarbons and amendments to the Geological and Mining Law, as – according to the government – the current regulations did not provide an adequate level of supervision over companies searching for shale gas in Poland. The proposed regulations guaranteed ownership rights to those who already possessed licences, such as the right to preferential access (without participation in a tender) to the mining usufruct for holders of exploration-licences who could document the existence of shale gas deposits (Malinowski 2012). The most significant change proposed at that time was the establishment of a new body called the National Operator of Energy Minerals (NOKE) (Malinowski 2012), whose role would be to participate in each company's exploration activities as a business partner to help build a sustainable, long-term hydrocarbon-based economy in Poland. It would not exert control over companies' activities, but it would assure a better flow of information between investors and the Ministry of Environment. Moreover, NOKE's participation in the application for an exploitation permit would not be mandatory but would depend on a company's individual decision (Mazurczak 2014). These policy proposals resulted from strategic resource security concerns which were their primary justification. Some even started speaking in terms of "Polish shale", meaning shale gas as a strategic resource that should be fully controlled by the Polish state. With the establishment of NOKE, the energy security frame moved to the forefront. At the same time, however, NOKE was the institution through which the security objectives of the government and the economic objectives of the companies were intended to align. This was the moment when some actors in the Polish government questioned the self-Orientalizing strategy of inviting foreign investors to provide capital for drilling through the Polish subsurface. The idea was to maintain state control over the process; to be a sovereign state. The year 2012 witnessed the peak of exploration activities, with 24 drilling operations completed. However, it was also in 2012 that one of the biggest players in the shale gas industry, ExxonMobil, withdrew from Poland. New questions emerged in public discourse: Was there shale gas hidden in the Polish subsoil or was there nothing to look and hope for? Why did ExxonMobil leave Poland if the initial assessments of the US EIA were so optimistic? Did the government do something wrong? Was the Polish state not welcoming enough to such a wealthy global player of the oil and gas sector? Was Poland not Oriental enough in providing structural conditions for foreign investors to feel comfortable there?

The familiar fear of Russia (Zarycki 2004) was also reignited, as some sensed a Russian plot behind ExxonMobil's withdrawl. And while local protests and local fears about possible environmental degradation had become more visible, it was the exit of this global oil and gas giant that turned out to be more significant for the political decisions of the Polish government. As a consequence, the Polish Prime Minister replaced the Minister of the Environment and gave a clear message to his cabinet that a faster pace for taxation legislation and easier licensing procedures were expected. Two pieces of legislation were finally adopted by Parliament in 2014 and in 2016 – the Law on Special Taxation of Hydrocarbons and an amendment to the Geological and Mining Law. The proposed legislation also changed concession fees which had been in place for the previous 40 years. According to an expert from the Institute of Energy Studies (ISE) in Warsaw, this change ruined the business plans of most of the companies that were searching for shale gas in Poland and made the whole enterprise much less profitable. Moreover, the new legislation came into force relatively late, at a time when the Polish shale gas project was already beginning to slow down, due mainly to low oil and gas prices on global markets and the geological difficulties of Polish shale rock. Furthermore, the uncertainty surrounding the final level of fees and the shape of other regulations was by that time causing a lot of confusion.

Environmental valuation of shale gas in the EU

In September 2012, the European Commission published three different reports which addressed both market and environmental impacts of unconventional hydrocarbons in the EU.[4] In November 2012, a high-level official from the Energy Security Unit of the European Commission and the JRC, Arne Eriksson, took part in a conference on Energy Security in Vilnus to argue that shale gas has already had a significant impact on the EU energy market, but that its role may be more about improving liquidity on European energy markets than about achieving the independence from particular suppliers. At this time the European Community's JRC was busy working on a number of analysis reports related to shale gas extraction.[5] All of these reports were based on data coming from the US, risk assessment methodologies or modelling and various recommended regulatory measures. However, at that time the European Commission was not sure what kind of legislative action to propose.

In order to understand what EU citizens thought about the development of unconventional hydrocarbons and what they expected from EU-level institutions, between 20 December 2012 and 23 March 2013, the DG Environment of the European Commission organized a public consultation called "Unconventional fossil fuels [i.e. shale gas] in Europe" in all official EU languages. The consultation "generated 22,875 responses, with citizen contributions accounting for more than 95 percent of the total. More than 90 percent of the citizen responses came from five EU countries: Poland, France, Romania, Spain and Germany. There were 696 responses from organisations, including 33 percent from companies and 32 percent from NGOs" (BIO Intelligence Service 2013, p. 13). The level of participation from Poland was the highest. Of the 22,122 individual participants, around half (11,714) were from Poland. It is anecdotal that the largest share of registered consultation participants had their e-mail addresses at pgnig.pl – the Polish state owned oil and gas company. According to some of my interviewees who were involved in this process, managers at PGNiG ordered their employees to fill in the consultation forms (Interview 2). Mobilization was high and the purpose was to provide a positive opinion about shale gas development in Europe.

The report presenting the consultation results concluded that "despite the divergence of personal opinions of individual respondents about the development of unconventional fossil fuels (e.g. shale gas) in general, a broad consensus emerges that: 'Measures are necessary to address the potential challenges of unconventional fossil fuels (e.g. shale gas); Transparency and information are necessary at all stages'" (BIO Intelligence Service 2013, p. 13). Therefore, despite such a high mobilization of PGNiG employees, the report concluded that "doing nothing" was the least-favoured option by the respondents and some adjustment of the existing framework was needed (BIO Intelligence Service 2013, p. 14). However, in the Impact Assessment report (European Commission 2014b), which came a year later, the Commission warned that only "when responses are weighted to reflect a country's population (five countries made up more than 90 percent of the individual responses), a strong majority is in favour of a comprehensive framework at EU level" (p. 4). Further on, it mentions without naming a specific country that "based on informal indications, one member state would prefer to rely only on national provisions, while · a number of member states see a need for EU action, ranging from guidance to amendments to existing EU legislation up to a stand-alone regulatory approach" (European Commission 2014b, p. 4). Apparently, this one member state was Poland and the European Commission used the weighting procedure to mask the outstanding mobilization of the Polish citizens who were opposed to the EU-level regulations. The situation was similar to the one described in the case of the ETS Directive negotiations, where the European Commission used a statistical average to hide the extreme impacts of the reformed emissions trading system on member state economies. In both cases, the scale of the EU policy action was constructed by the European Commission by means of statistical operations, in each case serving the same purpose – concealing the extremes.

Around 2012, the same DG started working on a draft directive regulating the shale gas industry as a separate entity – a separate mining and industrial activity. An assistant to a Polish MEPs provided me with a paper version of a draft directive. Our interview took place in 2015, when "shale gas fever" was slowly beginning to cool down. He told me that in 2012–2013 the draft was circulating between offices, raising fear among Polish delegates. They were afraid that the European Commission would make the shale gas project environmentally costly for companies. This would put an end to "cheap nature" and would have made investment in Poland less attractive for oil and gas companies. The situation calmed down in January 2014 when the Commission issued recommendations rather softly regulating some aspects of unconventional hydrocarbon extraction. According to the European Commission, the need for harmonized and consistent approaches at the EU level was expressed in Eurobarometer surveys in 2011 and 2013. The recommendation was assisted by an Impact Assessment study (European Commission 2014b), which predicted that commercial production could start in Poland in 2015–2017. Impacts listed in the report included risks related to the use and pollution of water; air emissions (including volatile organic compounds and methane); and community impacts such as land use, biodiversity, noise and traffic. The general objective of the recommendation was formulated to ensure that "unconventional fossil fuel developments, in particular shale gas, are carried out with proper climate and environmental safeguards in place and under the maximum legal clarity and predictability for responsible authorities, citizens and operators, thus enabling the development of the sector" (European Commission 2014b, p. 3).

Four legislative options were considered by the European Commission:

1. A recommendation to member states on ways of addressing the environmental aspects of shale gas exploration and production. This would provide guidance on the interpretation of environmental legislation (relating to matters such as water and waste). Moreover, it would encourage voluntary commitments by the sector's operators.
2. Amendments to some existing EU environmental legislation to clarify the applicable rules for the sector.
3. A framework directive proposing a set of overarching goals, including the disclosure of chemicals used and dealing with cumulative impacts, while amending the existing environmental legislation.
4. A directive setting specific requirements covering all the issues identified.

The first option would have generated the least cost for businesses and administrations. At the same time, the Commission's documents from 2014, like the Impact Assessment report, pointed to uncertainties in the estimated levels of shale gas resources in Europe. As the analysis below will show, this uncertainty could not have been reduced without doing actual operations underground. This, in turn, required huge investments of capital which companies were unwilling to commit in light of the legal uncertainties. There were thus various uncertainties distributed at so many various levels that it became difficult to proceed with the shale gas development project in the EU.

Scaling up Polish expertise on shale gas: from seven local studies to the EU-level expertise

In 2010, the Ministry of the Environment, through one of its agencies, the Directorate-General Directorate for Environmental Protectio, commissioned the first study that would examine whether companies extracting shale gas in Poland were abiding by the rules and administrative procedures regulating mining activities. The study was carried out by the Polish Geological Institute (PGI) and focused mostly on administrative side of the project; it did not measure the impacts of exploration on the environment. The first empirical study on the environmental impacts of shale gas extraction was also commissioned by the DGEP and was carried out by the PGI at a site called Łebień. The study resulted in a report that was published in March 2012. It did not reveal any negative impacts of hydraulic fracturing on water or soil (PGI 2011). The Łebień Report was translated into English and is available from the PGI's website in both Polish and English (PGI 2011). PGI experts presented the results of their study to the JRC in Brussels in 2013, and geological services from other EU member states were made aware of it. However, as the Polish geologists recall, none of the country representatives showed interest in the report beyond that meeting (Interview 3). There were no questions posed by German or Dutch colleagues, for example. Despite this one-time appearance, according to them, the Ministry did not make nearly enough use of the report in political arenas – neither in Poland nor with other European countries or EU institutions in Brussels. Therefore, in terms of scaling up this piece of Polish expertise, some effort was made but the results were rather poor – the report appeared in policy arenas outside of Poland but was never inscribed or institutionalized as a European piece of expertise. As such, it was an object of discussion but not a part of the institutional practices of Brussels policy actors. Some Polish MEPs enquired in the European Parliament about the reasons why the reports had not been referred to in the shale gas debate at the EU level. And although the Director of DG Environment visited the Łebień exploration site (Makuch 2014, p. 249), remained Orientalized as expertise not relevant to the EU-level deliberation.

Polish geologists were also involved in reviewing the EU-level expertise. The Ministry of the Environment asked PGI experts for their opinions on studies commissioned by the European Commission. The response that came was very critical. Geologists from PGI pointed out that no empirical measurements had been taken to provide grounds for the conclusions of the studies. That report, as one expert interviewed by me pointed out, "was merely based on the authors' opinions" (Interview 4). To illustrate the difference between the approach adopted in the reviewed reports and in the report prepared by the PGI, the expert made a comment about the characteristics of post-fracking fluids: "We do not say that post-fracking fluids should not be spilled over the fields because we don't like it. We are saying that this should not be done because we measured the chemical content of this fluid" (Interview 4). The reaction was similar for seismic activity: "These things need to be measured, otherwise all conclusions become pure, worthless speculations" (Interview 4). However, these comments remained local and did not change the logic of impact assessment or risk assessment studies at the EU level. Even if Polish experts tried to question the logic of environmental investigations into the impacts of fracking practices in EU institutions, this logic remained intact and the relation between who is reviewed (East) and who does the reviewing (West) did not change.

In the summer of 2013, the PGI presented the results from another study that had been carried out at seven different fracking locations. When looking at the content of the report, one can see that several types of environmental impacts were analysed there: both the actual as well as the potential impacts of hydraulic fracturing on the atmosphere with regard to the content of hydrocarbons, radon and dust, and on land surface and soil with regard to agricultural production and the content of hydrocarbons, as well as surface and underground waters (PGI 2015, p. 9). The PGI also examined samples of fracking fluids, as well as solid and fluid post-fracking waste, for the presence of toxic substances. Experts from the PGI also took samples of the extracted gas in order to measure its chemical content and describe its isotope characteristics. While PGI experts managed to conduct a baseline study (i.e. to describe the state of the environment before fracking operations began) at two of the seven study locations – Wysin and Zawada – at the other five locations PGI researchers carried out their measurements only after the wells had been drilled or hydraulic fracturing had begun. Additionally, after the exploration works had been closed, PGI experts measured levels of noise and emissions into the atmosphere and examined the state of the environment after one of the companies re-cultivated the exploration site. PGI's research operations at each site depended on the type of contract it signed with the company and on the company's willingness to coordinate its operations with the work of the PGI experts. The 2014 report would thus not have been possible without the cooperation of companies, as the production of expertise on the environmental impacts of shale gas extraction depended on the investment of capital into subsoil operations and the kinds of relations that could only be established between experts and companies' management.

At the same time, for security reasons, the names of drilling sites were classified by a government security agency. PGI experts were not able to obtain any clarification from the government for the reasons behind this extraordinary measure, which made it difficult for them to conduct their fieldwork. While collecting soil and water samples in the studied locations, experts were not able to explain to the local people what they were doing and for what purpose. This gave rise to some distrust around their activities and people began to suspect that the government was doing something towards shale gas extraction in secret and against the will of its citizens. As we can see, while it seemed necessary for the state agencies and the PGI to strike alliances with companies, it seemed less vital to have open and trusting relations with the inhabitants of the studied locations. On a practical level, good relations with the local people were helpful for the experts' activities, but at the institutional level, at the level of state politics, these people seemed redundant or even potentially disruptive to expertise production. This security measure may be interpreted as Orientalization of its own citizens by the state. Citizens were not approached as equal partners but rather as potential obstructers, that did not understand and could bring harm to the process of expertise production and, ultimately, to shale gas development.

However, the alliance between the PGI and the companies, especially those representing foreign capital, was fragile as well. This fragility was discovered by the Supreme Chamber of Control, which controlled the work of the public institutions related to shale gas development (the Ministries and the PGI). The control was commissioned by the former Chief Country Geologist (2005–2007) and supported by the Parliamentary Team for Resources and Energy. According to the produced report, the PGI was not well enough prepared to properly archive rock materials that companies were obliged to share with the state. Companies would deliver samples of shale rock and the PGI would not be able to verify its quality. According to the report of the Supreme Audit Office on "Granting Licences to Explore Reserves of Copper and Hydrocarbons, Including Unconventional Hydrocarbons" (NIK 2016) and the former Chief Country Geologist, valuable samples were transported by foreign companies to the US and Germany (Makuch 2014, p. 134) and the PGI was left with low-quality leftover rocks, often cut into pieces that were not useful for assessing volumes of the resource underground. This illustrates well the structural dependency of Polish geological experts on companies with regard to knowledge production. It seems that access to capital was not only vital in order to make more precise assessments about the volumes of extractable resource, but it was also important for being able to hold the capital in place, for containing it within the state institutions, and for using it for the production of expertise over time. According to Jędrysek (Makuch 2014), exploration activities were followed by geological information trading which was completely obscured from the view of public authorities who were unable to determine "who has what types of information, how this information was accessed by some actors and what they have done with it" (p. 135). To a large extent, state institutions lost control over knowledge about the country's subsoil.

In all these complex relations, the PGI experts saw their role mainly as the suppliers of reliable and objective knowledge that was not "poisoned" with invested interests: "We are just saying how things are, what comes out of the measurements. And knowledge is needed at each stage of the shale gas development project" (Interview 4). The head of one of the PGI departments was of the opinion that all regulations should rely on solid research results. The weakness of relying on a small data sample, as pointed out by the critics of the PGi's reports, was seen as a strength by the PGI experts themselves. The methodological superiority of the PGI's studies as compared to other studies prepared at that time by different institutions in Europe (mainly Germany) was in the systematically collected empirical evidence. As the PGI's high-level expert pointed out:

> It is very bad if regulations are based on convictions or opinions, even if these are computer models, with all due respect for computer modelling or this what is called assessment. Risk assessment is based on some hypothetical assumptions about risks and the reality. Empirical studies are based on an analysis of empirical facts. A necessary requirement for any good geological study is to take into account the specificities of local geological conditions.
>
> (Interview 4)

However, modelling seemed to be the methodology of the West in the shale gas debate. Moreover, it helps to scale-up expertise beyond particular locations, and it helps to operate on abstractions that can be generalized to different contexts. Modelling helps to build scenarios and move beyond particular statements that X and Y impacts were or were not observed in a Z location at a given moment in time. Specific case studies based on local measurements give knowledge about single locations only. It is not easy to scale them up, to make them relevant for other locations, for all EU member states. According to the geological experts from the PGI, different kinds of regulations should be proposed in Poland, in China and in the USA or Argentina, because each of these countries has completely different geological conditions. While some areas may be seismically active, others will never be at risk of earthquakes. The PGI's report, according to the geologists, took these local conditions into account and the baseline measurements gave an idea about the state of the environment prior to hydraulic fracturing.

However, the logic of deliberation, expertise production and policy-making at the EU level seemed to be different. It was about finding common denominators, shared perspectives and common solutions. An EU-level policy would need to accommodate local differences if it was to be accepted by all, and focusing on particularities seemed to be a step in the wrong direction. At the same time, even though the PGI report (2015) presented results from just seven local studies, the Ministry "was taking the PGI reports everywhere it went and was referring to their results in each and every discussion about shale gas regulations" (Interview 3). One of the main PGI experts pointed out that the PGI studies are of unique value in Europe, perhaps even worldwide. No such study with baseline measurements of the condition of the environment had ever before been carried out in the US, which made it difficult to precisely measure the impact of hydraulic fracturing on environment there. No one else was drilling in Europe, and thus no one else was able to measure the impacts of hydraulic fracturing on the environment.

Meanwhile, as mentioned previously in this chapter, the European Commission saw it as important to produce expertise on shale gas and other unconventional fossil fuels. One of the first indications of this need can be found in the resolution of the European Parliament from November 2012 (European Parliament 2012). The resolution calls for the establishment of an "independent platform" that would assemble industry and science representatives who would be asked to "provide opinions and establish good practices related to clean shale gas extraction technologies". The idea for a pan-European "platform" or "network" subsequently took shape in a sequence of policy documents, despite the fact that its envisaged objectives received mixed feedback from stakeholders during a meeting organized by the JRC in Madrid, 7–8 March 2013 (Eriksson et al. 2013). However, the decision to establish a more permanent body of experts was nevertheless approved after this meeting, although it took until July 2014 for the UH Network to be publicly launched with its proper name and agenda (see Lis et al. 2019).

The aim of the network was initially envisaged as "increasing our knowledge on unconventional hydrocarbon extraction technologies and practices also in order to further reduce potential health and environmental impacts and risks" (European Commission 2014a). In the Communication, the future network was further promoted as a facilitator for "open and transparent" information sharing with the public. More precisely, the Commission announced that it "will establish a European Science and Technology Network on Unconventional Hydrocarbon Extraction, bringing together practitioners from industry, research, academia as well as civil society" (European Commission

2014a). As the document puts it, the primary objective of the network was to "collect, analyse and review results from exploration projects, as well as to assess the development of technologies used in unconventional gas and oil projects" (European Commission 2014a). This would be the first attempt to collect data about the European experience with unconventional fossil fuels. Following the official launch of the UH Network in July 2014, this formulation was further expanded and adopted as the official mandate of the network. Specifically, the mandate describes the network's objectives as:

- Structuring the dialogue among the stakeholders, fostering open information and knowledge sharing;
- Presenting and discussing research activities and their results, as well as identifying gaps and R&D needs;
- Examining knowledge gained from exploration and demonstration projects;
- Identifying and assessing emerging technologies including their economic, environment and climate impacts.

(Mandate... 2014, p. 1)

One of the main challenges that had to be faced in relation to the assumed goals was that of data collection itself. The Network Steering Committee did not want to rely on data coming from outside of Europe – for example, the USA or China – as the goal was to present the European experience with unconventional hydrocarbons through data on environmental impacts and emerging technologies. Irrespective of various misunderstandings among Network members as to the status of "objective data" and "politics", "the universals" and "the particulars" (Choy 2011), the essential problem was constituted by the fact that the number of fracking operations for the exploration or extraction of unconventional hydrocarbons in Europe was very low at that time. Around 20 shale gas extraction operations in Poland and a few more in the Netherlands and in the UK made up a very limited on-the-ground experience from which any data could be retrieved. This could have been offset with data about tight gas extraction, but the issue of real importance for the public was that of shale oil and gas extraction.

Despite generous representation from companies such as ExxonMobil and active participation of industry leaders at Network meetings in between meetings the main burden of data collection fell on the shoulders of the Network Chairpersons. Companies were eager to share data that were already public and the Chairpersons were most effective in obtaining information from public institutions. Thus, interestingly, despite accusations coming from the Brussels NGO's that the European Commission favoured the shale industry, knowledge that was accessible for the Commission representatives was mainly accumulated in public domains (Lis et al. 2019). Moreover, the relation between public institutions and companies involved in knowledge production by underground exploration of shale rock formations was organized at the level of member states, and the European Commission was not able to interfere in it. Commission representatives and the Network's Steering Committee members were only able to access knowledge that became public at the level of nation states as a result of negotiations between state and capital.

One of the high-level experts of the Polish Geological Institute was invited to join the Network's Steering Committee. He was happy to tell me in an interview that the CEO of the Polish oil and gas company PGNiG publicly announced that they would make their data accessible to the Network (Interview 3). However, the main input from Poland came from the PGI itself, and more specifically, from the study of the environmental impact assessment of hydraulic fracturing on the seven locations in Poland that I have already described. In fact, most of the data which was accumulated and later added to a database aimed at representing "the European shale gas experience" came from Polish studies. This did not happen automatically, however. Before the data generated by the Polish experts in geology could be added to the database , the European Commission decided that the PGI studies needed to be reviewed by European experts. The review was carried out by experts from the European Commission's JRC, who presented their comments during one of the Working Group meetings of the UH Network. Again the West reviewed the East and this time, in this configuration, the review was successful at scaling up a piece of expertise. The review was positive and the Polish data, gathered by the PGI from seven different locations in Poland, was inserted into the database representing the European experience with shale gas extraction. Five of the studied locations were declassified only in 2015 prior to a conference that took place in Brussels in September 2015. Conclusions from the PGI reports were presented to the European public at that meeting and, as the PGI experts explained, it would have made little sense to discuss results from a local empirical study without disclosing the names of the seven locations.

A high-level expert from the PGI was satisfied with the review and the contribution of his institution to the European debate. He was of the opinion that sharing the Polish experience with other countries was a valuable thing to do, as other countries would be able to make their own decisions, having studied whether it had been beneficial for Poland to explore shale gas potential or not. Even though conditions are different for each country, the Polish experience would provide a benchmark for how things may have developed in the particular Polish context. He thought of Poland's role as a pioneering work: "a pioneer always bears more costs and this time Poland is a pioneer of shale extraction in Europe" (Interview 4). Thus, through the UH Network that was initiated and organized by European institutions, the PGI reports finally gained relevance for the EU-level debates on shale gas, and the expertise on shale gas produced in Poland was inscribed into a database that represented "the European experience with unconventional hydrocarbons". Through relations with EU-level actors, through participation in an EU-level network of experts, the scaling-up of the PGI's expertise was eventually possible and expertise produced in Poland was de-Orientalized.

Conclusions

As the study shows, production of knowledge about the subsoil is highly contingent on capital, which needs to be invested in the underground operations necessary for obtaining any information about the characteristics of a resource. The capitalism-in-nature and nature-in-capitalism double internality thus also involves knowledge-in-capitalism and capitalism-in-knowledge internality. States and regional para-state governance structures such as the EU, within which nature is exploited by capital, not only work to attract capital for the exploration of "nature"but also need to strike cooperation with companies when they want to gain more expertise about the resource and the impacts of its exploitation. This happened both at the state level – as exemplified by the need of the PGI to form alliances with companies in order to carry out measurements of soil, water, noise and air quality at the licensed sites – and at the EU level – as seen in the case of the UH Network officials trying to collect data on technical and environmental aspects of shale gas projects in Europe.

At the same time, as the chapter shows, in order to gain leverage at the EU level, Polish state institutions, including PGI, had to start operating within the institutional arena of the EU. The capacity to produce expertise at the state level, within the means of state agencies and their resources, was not sufficient to make domestic expertise relevant at the EU level. Only through the incorporation of high-level PGI experts and through the review of the PGI's reports by JRC experts did the Polish expertise gain relevance and was inscribed into the

EU-level institutional politics around shale gas and other unconventional resources extractions, becoming de-Orientalized.

Notes

1 Initial drilling and fracking operations had revealed that the composition of Polish shale rock is different from that found in the USA. It is located much deeper underground and it also contains clay, which makes gas extraction less efficient. For these reasons it was more difficult to transfer existing hydraulic fracturing technology from the US to Poland.
2 www.ncbr.gov.pl/programy/programy-krajowe/wspolne-przedsiewziecia/blue-gas-polski-gaz-lupkowy/
3 www.ncbr.gov.pl/index.php?id=31329&L=0%23a86_u1%23a101_u1%27%20and%202077%3D2077%27-&tx_news_pi1%5Bnews%5D=44999&cHash=677a7e81e510228456c5bcd458bfc53f
4 The DG Energy in cooperation with the JRC issued an analysis report titled "Unconventional gas: potential energy market impacts in the EU" (DG Energy/JRC 2012), the DG Climate published "Climate Impact of potential shale gas production in the EU" (DG Climate 2012) and the DG Environment published "Support for the identification of potential risks for the environment and human health arising from hydrocarbons operations involving hydraulic fracturing in Europe" (DG Environment 2012).
5 Activities at JRC included: (1) Institute for Energy and Transport: "Unconventional gas: potential energy market impacts in the EU", "Best available technology" and "Wider economic implications of domestic shale gas"; (2) Institute for Environment and Sustainability: "Study focused on land use and water demand" and "Literature review report on environmental and social impacts"; (3) Institute for Prospective Technological Studies: "Review of best available technologies reports (BREFs, Mining Waster Directive)"; (4) Institute for Health and Consumer Protection: "Review of REACH registration dossiers for fracturing fluid additives".

References

Choy, T. (2011) *Ecologies of Comparison: An Ethnography of Endangerment in Hong Kong*. Durham, NC: Duke University Press.
Fougner, T. (2006) The state, international competitiveness and neoliberal globalization: is there a future beyond 'the competition state'? *Review of International Studies* 32: 165–185.
Kama, K. (2019) Resource-making controversies: knowledge, anticipatory politics and economization of unconventional fossil fuels. *Progress in Human Geography*. https://doi.org/10.1177/0309132519829223
Lis, A., Kama, K. and Reins, L. (2019) Co-production European knowledge and publics amidst controversy: the EU expert network on unconventional hydrocarbons. *Science and Public Policy* 46(5): 721–731.

Lis, A. and Stankiewicz, P. (2017) Framing shale gas for policy-making in Poland. *Journal of Environmental Policy and Planning* 19(1): 53–71.

Moore, J. W. (2015) *Capitalism in the Web of Life: Ecology and the Accumulation of Capital.* London: Verso.

Zarycki, T. (2004) Uses of Russia: The role of Russia in the modern Polish national identity. *East European Politics & Societies* 18(4): 595–627.

Documents

BIO Intelligence Service (2013) Analysis and presentation of the results of the public consultation "Unconventional fossil fuels (e.g. shale gas) in Europe". European Commission DG Environment. Retrieved 2 March 2018 from https://ec.europa.eu/environment/integration/energy/pdf/Shale%20gas%20consultation_report.pdf

DG Climate (2012) *Climate impact of potential shale gas production in the EU.* Brussels: AEA Technology. Retrieved 5 March 2013 from https://ec.europa.eu/clima/sites/clima/files/eccp/docs/120815_final_report_en.pdf

DG Energy/JRC (2012) *Unconventional gas: potential energy market impacts in the EU.* Brussels: European Commission/Joint Research Centre/Institute for Energy and Transport. Retrieved 5 March 2013 from www.researchgate.net/publication/267269691_Unconventional_Gas_Potential_Energy_Market_Impacts_in_the_European_Union

DG Environment (2012) *Support for the identification of potential risks for the environment and human health arising from hydrocarbons operations involving hydraulic fracturing in Europe.* Brussels: AEA Technology. Retrieved 5 March 2013 from https://ec.europa.eu/environment/integration/energy/pdf/fracking%20study.pdf

Energy Information Administration (EIA) (2011) *World Shale Gas Resources: An Initial Assessment of 14 Regions Outside the United States.* Retrieved 14 January 2014 from www.eia.gov/analysis/studies/worldshalegas/archive/2011/pdf/fullreport.pdf

Eriksson, A., Gandossi, L. and Zeniewski, P. (2013) Workshop Proceedings: Safe and Efficient Shale Gas Exploration and Production, Reference Report, the Joint Research Centre of the European Commission. Retrieved 4 April 2020 from http://publications.jrc.ec.europa.eu/repository/bitstream/JRC82564/ld-na-25990-en-n.pdf

European Commission (2014a) Commission Communication on the exploration and production of hydrocarbons (such as shale gas) using high volume hydraulic fracturing in the EU. COM(2014)23 final/2. Brussels, 17 March 2014.

European Commission (2014b) Impact Assessment report accompanying the document Communication from the Commission to the European Parliament, the Council, the European Economic and Social Committee of the Regions: Exploration and production of hydrocarbons (such as shale gas) using high volume hydraulic fracturing in the EU. COM(2014)23 final.

European Parliament (2012) Resolution of 21 November 2012 on industrial, energy and other aspects of shale gas and oil. Retrieved 27 January 2020 from www.europarl.europa.eu/sides/getDoc.do?type=TA& reference=P7-TA-2012-0444&language=EN

Mandate of the European Science and Technology Network on Unconventional Hydrocarbon Extraction (7 July 2014) Ares(2014)4022184 – 02/12/2014. Retrieved 28 May 2015 from https://ec.europa.eu/jrc/sites/jrcsh/files/Mandate_and_ROP_attached_to_note_to_JS.PDF

NIK (2016) *Report on Granting Licences to Explore Reserves of Copper and Hydrocarbons, Including Unconventional Hydrocarbons.* Warsaw: Supreme Audit Office. Retrieved 20 January 2020 from www.nik.gov.pl/plik/id,15574,vp,18057.pdf

PGI (2011) *Badania aspektów środowiskowych procesu szczelinowania hydraulicznego wykonanego w otworze Łebień LE-2H [The Study of Environmental Aspects of Hydraulic Fracturing on the Borehole Łebień LE-2H].* Warsaw: Polish Geological Institute.

PGI (2012) *Ocena Zasobów Wydobywalnych Gazu Ziemnego i Ropy Naftowej w Formacjach Łupkowych Dolnego Paleozoiku w Polsce (Basen Bałtycko-Podlasko-Lubleski) [Assessment of extractable Natural Gas and Oil Resources in Shale Formation of the Lower Paleozoic in Poland (the Baltic-Podlasie-Lubelskie Basin)].* Warsaw: Polish Geological Institute. Retrieved 3 March 2018 from www.pgi.gov.pl/docman-tree/aktualnosci-2012/zasoby-gazu/771-raport-pl/file.html

PGI (2015) *Środowisko i prace rozpoznawcze dotyczące gazu z łupków. Wyniki badań środowiska gruntowo-wodnego, powietrza, klimatu akustycznego, płynów technologicznych i odpadów [Environment and Shale Gas Exploration. Results from the Study of Soil, Water, Air, Noise, Produced Fluids and Waste].* Warsaw: Ministry of Environment/General Directorate for Environmental Protection. https://doi.org/10.13140/RG.2.2.23326.95042

Media Reports

Górlikowski, M. (2013) Jak gaz łupkowy zmienia pomorskie Lubocino. *Gazeta Wyborcza* (30 May 2013). Retrieved from http://wyborcza.pl/1,155287,13941208,Jak_gaz_lupkowy_zmienia_pomorskie_Lubocino.html

Makuch. G. (2014) Gaz Łupkowy: Wielka gra o bezpieczeństwo energetyczne [Shale gas: a great game for energy security].

Malinowski, D. (2012) Po co w gazie łupkowym Narodowy Operator Kopalin Energetycznych? [Why do we need a National Operator of Fossil Fuels?]. *WNP*. Retrieved 3 March 2014 from http://gazownictwo.wnp.pl/po-co-w-gazie-lupkowym-narodowyoperatorkopalin-energetycznych,181697_1_0_0.html

Mazurczak, M. (2014) Bez NOKE polski sektor łupkowy to europejskie Eldorado [Without NOKE, the Polish shale gas Eldorado becomes a

European Eldorado]. *Łupki Polskie*. Retrieved 3 March 2014 from http://gazlupkowy.pl/bez-noke-polski-sektor-lupkowy-to-europejskie-eldorado/

Interviews

Interview 1: Expert at ISE, Warsaw, September 2015.

Interview 2: Expert at PGNiG, Warsaw, September 2015.

Interview 3: Expert at PGI, Warsaw, July 2017.

Interview 4: Expert at PGI, September, 2015.

4 Co-production of sociopolitical orders
Energy objects, publics and states

Introduction

This chapter describes the processes through which objectification of carbon dioxide and shale gas co-produced broader sociopolitical orders in terms of the relations between states and publics. The first part of the chapter focuses on the co-production of new categories of workers along a scale of "cleanness", on which different jobs may be positioned as "clean/green" and "dirty/black" depending on the amount of carbon dioxide that is emitted based on the work done by humans and machines together. Existing human and machine constellations at different production sites had to begin to account for a new actor – carbon dioxide emissions. The existence or non-existence as well as the intensity of this object in production processes started to matter when jobs were compared, valued, saved or abandoned. Carbon dioxide as a greenhouse gas introduced a new political dimension to the discussion about jobs in Europe and, in this chapter, I examine how trade union representatives from Poland negotiated their own presence on a new scale of clean and dirty jobs.

In the second part of the chapter, I analyse how shale gas politics co-produced different publics on different scales, local, regional, national and European, and how within these publics various relations between states and citizens were negotiated. Shale gas as an object was not only constructed and co-produced by experts, administrations and companies; it was also objectified (and sometimes objected to) by local communities in various parts of Poland. Being strongly politicized by the Polish government of the time, shale gas entered public debate in media and in local conversations in many communities loaded with hopes and fears. Its potential presence was felt even more strongly when companies began to arrive with heavy equipment ready to explore the local subsoil. Two issues are at stake in the analysis which unfolds in this chapter.

First, I aim to understand how shale gas as an object established new terrains within which relations between the Polish state and its citizens were negotiated with respect to energy politics. Second, I want to problematize how the visibility and invisibility of various objects, actors and processes became important in structuring relations between citizens and the state. As the shale gas development project unfolded in various operations carried out by companies, yet another object became politicized among local inhabitants: post-fracking waste. Its visibility and invisibility, and its association and disassociation with shale gas exploration in Poland, shaped relations of trust and mistrust between Polish citizens and state institutions.

Carbon dioxide and the scalar politics of European labour

In March 2008 the European Trade Union Confederation (ETUC) supported the European Commission's proposal of the Climate Change and Energy Package with its goals of 20 percent reductions in carbon dioxide emissions (from 1990 levels), a 20 percent share of renewable energy sources in Europe's energy mix and a 20 percent increase in energy efficiency within the European Union by 2020 (ETUC 2008). ETUC offered its support under certain conditions. In the first paragraph of its position statament, it stated that the EU must take the lead in climate change action and "transform emissions reduction into an opportunity to create quality jobs and lessen social inequalities" (ETUC 2008, p. 1). In this way, carbon dioxide emissions entered politics in relation to labour and people's livelihoods, reshuffling the existing categories of jobs and also, potentially, the employment map of the EU. Once carbon dioxide became a visible and costly part of the production processes, its disappearance and its reduction would mean mass unemployment in some industries where new technologies would not make the production process any cleaner. In the ETUC's position statement, jobs in polluting and carbon-intensive industries were called "dirty", while jobs in low-carbon industries were framed as "green". The ETUC predicted that many workers and their families would lose their livelihoods due to emission reduction in the EU (ETUC 2008, p. 1–2), as dirty jobs would have to disappear.

Along this new scale of jobs – from dirty to clean, from black to green – the ETUC scaled various economic areas according to their ability to lower carbon dioxide emissions in industry. Thus, the ETUC demanded that the EU introduce border tax adjustments for products imported from countries with no greenhouse gas reduction policies. The logic behind this request was two-fold. Firstly, the ETUC wanted to keep European goods globally competitive as compared with goods produced in "dirty" regions such as Central Asia or China, and thus prevent Europe from being flooded with cheap and unsustainably produced goods. Secondly, the ETUC was afraid that if, after 2012, industries received allowances (EUAs) for free, some of them would sell their EUAs on the ETS and move their production processes outside of Europe to regions where greenhouse gas emissions did not constitute a production cost. The mobility of capital was thus taken into account as a major concern for immobile workers whose livelihoods tied to particular jobs, industries or locations – and thus carbon dioxide emissions.

In order to ensure that the interests of workers were well represented in climate debates, the ETUC asked for "the establishment of a consultative committee of the European social partners on the energy–climate change package" (ETUC 2008, p. 1). The ETUC argued for regular and binding consultations with European social partners, which would be "obligatory, under the Emission trading directive" (ETUC 2008, p. 2) and a "just employment transition", financially supported by social impact mitigation programmes. After a series of in-house consultations, the position paper on the Climate Change and Energy Package was adopted by the Executive Committee of the ETUC at its meeting of 4 March 2008 in Brussels. It was accepted and signed by all national affiliates of the ETUC, including three Polish national trade union organizations: the Trade Unions' Forum (FZZ), the All-Poland Alliance of Trade Unions (OPZZ) and the Independent Self-Governing Trade Union Solidarność (NSZZ Solidarność). At that meeting, NSZZ Solidarność was represented by Andrzej Adamczyk from the National Commission in Gdańsk. In an interview with me in November 2008, he said that the ETUC's position statement, according to him, "had all it needed". He agreed with the ETUC's strong support for European climate policies and remarked that greenhouse gas reductions had to be undertaken as quickly as possible, in order to avoid a global climate disaster.

However, not all members of the ETUC, not even of Solidarność, shared these views. Despite an early and unanimous (no veto vote) adoption of the ETUC by its Executive Committee, some unions did not approve of the way the ETUC supported the Commission's proposal. The main actors reinvigorating this debate were the European Metalworkers' Federation (EMF), the European Mine, Chemical and Energy Workers Federation (EMCEF), German unions representing mining, chemical and energy workers, including IG Bergbau, Chemie, Energie (IG BCE), and Polish unions representing miners and energy workers, including SGiE Solidarność (Secretariat of Mining and Energy

Workers) and ZZG (Miners' Trade Union). Unions representing workers in European industries feared "carbon leakage", which would also mean "employment leakage" from Europe to "dirty" regions. However, unlike the capital that would flee the EU together with the carbon dioxide emitted by production processes, the employees (workers) would remain in the EU as a surplus population, adding possibly thousands of people to the category of unemployed European citizens. Unions representing workers from the power and mining sectors feared unemployment due to a gradual phase-out of coal from electricity generation in Europe and the closing of coal-fired power plants. In the case of these sectors, emissions would disappear together with the power plants and huge numbers of people would become unemplpyed.

The harshest criticisms of the ETUC's position came from the leader of the Secretariat of Mining and Energy Workers of Solidarność in Katowice (SGiE), Kazimierz Grajcarek and the expert from the National Commission of Solidarność in Gdańsk, a member of the Working Group on Sustainable Development. Dominik Kolorz from the miners' union Solidarność SKGWK (*Krajowy Sekretariat Górnictwa i Energetyki*) was also a prominent critic of the ETUC and European climate policies in general. Outside of the Solidarność union, Andrzej Chwiluk from the miners' union ZZG (*Związek Zawodowy Górników*), and Vice-President of EMCEF at that time, was also critical of the proposed climate legislation. In general they objected to the ETUC's overly hasty endorsement of the new package of legislation, and in particular for supporting full auctions for the power sector. While the ETUC proposed free allocation based on technological benchmarks for industries, as mentioned above, it accepted full auctions for the power sector as a fair solution. The criticisms that came from Solidarność reflected the calls of the Polish government and businesses upon EU policy-makers to account for early emission reductions in CEE countries from the 1990s. These reductions had cost Polish society massive job losses and poverty in de-industrialized regions. The lesson had been learned and the link between disappearing carbon dioxide emissions and disappearing jobs had had devastating implications. A similar threat, according to Solidarność officials, had to be considered as a possibility of the ETS.

Carbon dioxide appeared to my interviewees as a historical entity, an entity with a history. Carbon dioxide reductions were intertwined with a transition to market economies in the post-socialist countries in Europe. During the interviews I carried out with Solidarność officials, one argument was constantly repeated: EU member states cannot be forced to reduce carbon dioxide emissions at the same pace. They should be allowed to enter onto reduction paths individually. It was thus noted that carbon dioxide was deeply involved in many economic and social processes and its rapid reduction would change these significantly. Most importantly, disentanglement and reduction of carbon dioxide was seen as socially and economically very costly. At the same time, my interviewees tended to lean towards climate change denial. They didn't trust climate science or the Intergovernmental Panel for Climate Change as a body for reviewing the former.

Since the ETUC refused to revise its position according to the wishes of Polish union leaders, SGiE Solidarność set out to look for support from European industry federations. The SGiE leader turned to the EMCEF, of which SGiE and ZZG were members. The EMCEF had already been working on the Climate Change and Energy Package and had also already asked the ETUC to revise its position. In early October 2008, two positions on the Climate Change and Energy Package were adopted – one at the Coordination Council of the EMCEF in Katowice and the other three days later at the National Congress of Solidarność in Wadowice. The first one was written in Katowice by the Coordination Council of EMCEF attended by Erik Macak, Secretary of the EMCEF, Józef Niemiec, Confederal Secretary of the ETUC, and representatives of the EMCEF Coordination Council Poland. This was the moment when the Polish case became the case of European industry union federations. The Eastern battle became a European one, and the signatures of Western colleagues were crucial for this transformation's realization. The signatories warned that the Climate Change and Energy Package would lead to:

- a rapid increase in electricity and heating prices in Europe;
- a closing down of the European power industry based on coal;
- importation of electricity from outside of the EU;
- auctions for carbon dioxide emission allowances after 2012 for the cement, lime, smelting, coke and glass industries, which would lead to mass imports of these products from outside the EU and a ceasing of investments in these industries within the EU;
- mass layoffs of workers in European industries (1 million jobs lost).

(EMCEF 2008)

The last two paragraphs urged

> the EMCEF and the ETUC to solicit for legislative solutions in the Climate Change and Energy Package that will include the specificity of the economies in the countries, which energy production

to a large extent depends on coal (in Poland 95% of electricity is produced from coal).

(EMCEF 2008)

During the December Summit of 2008, the final decisions concerning the Climate Change and Energy Package were taken by the European Heads of State. This included decisions on the new ETS Directive. Apart from the benchmarking allocation for emission allowances for European industries, none of the ETUC's demands were met. A requirement for regular consultations with social partners was not included in the text of the ETS Directive. A separate fund or financing mechanism for fair transition programmes was also not established. Neither were border tax adjustments on goods produced outside of the EU introduced (see Directive 2009/29/EC). In other words, the ETUC did not gain anything substantial in this round of negotiations.

This was a setback for the ETUC, but it was not a big surprise. All of my interviewees, including the advisor to the ETUC's Secretary, admitted that the ETUC had had a weak position within the EU arena for a long time. The Commission was willing to listen to industries, but usually ignored the stance of the unions. Apart from the Commissioner for Employment, Vladimir Spidla, who, according to my interviewees, was not a strong fighter for the unions' interests in any case, no one was interested in pushing through the unions' agenda. Externalities produced by the ETS carbon market – including unemployment – were left to be dealt with by national governments. The Advisor to the Secretary of the ETUC told me that she had seen some possibilities of the ETUC getting what it had asked for in 2008. Unfortunately, none of the promises ever turned into concrete decisions (Interview 1).

Negotiations for policies for carbon dioxide emission reductions forced European labour organizations to re-establish their position within the EU arena, and to search for partners with whom they would be able to scale up their voice. However, the weakness of the European labour movement at that time was beyond question and became even more visible against the privileged position that businesses had managed to win in the 2008 ETS negotiations. The business lobby, represented by the Zero Emissions Platform gathering oil- and coal-related companies, producers of equipment for those sectors and research institutes, managed to insert a line into the ETS Directive which stated that an equivalent of 300 million emission allowances would be put aside to finance the construction of carbon capture and storage (CCS) demonstration installations in the EU. This meant allocating auction revenues to companies for the sake of developing a technology which was not yet economically viable, and, more significantly, not necessarily environmentally friendly. The funds raised from auctioning off these 300 million emission allowances would be allocated to particular CCS projects in the EU. This finance mechanism was given its own name – NER300.

While getting actual money allocated to "just transition" in the EU seemed like a big challenge for European trade unions, which were more optimistic about the possibility of having an official consultative body established to discuss climate policies. The ETUC expert commented on the unions' failure in this issue as follows:

> And the other one was this consultative committee of social partners, which was probably easier to have. We have experience with that in Europe, e.g. in Spain, where social partners gather together at a social dialogue table to look at the employment part of the implementation of the Kyoto Protocol. This helps them to make the transition. I think it smooths out difficulties which arise when they have to take strong decisions. And we said to the Commission – we want something like that – because at the moment trade unions are not really involved in it. You have an easy relationship with industry, NGOs are very close to you, but unions are not really involved. And then we got informal and oral commitments from two commissioners Dimas and Spidla. We had a meeting with John Monks, the President of the ETUC, and the two commissioners were saying "we are going to set up a small group of people to explore what we can do, how we can set up this, etc." and this never happened. The working group was not set up. And all the civil servants, from the DG Environment in particular said that they opposed this idea.
>
> (Interview 1)

I asked the Secretary advisor from the ETUC why all the civil servants from the DG Environment would be against the idea, and she answered:

> Because there was this European Climate Change Program group and they were convinced that the consultation in the DG Environment was working well. They don't need us. To be frank, they don't see why we exist … or they need us only when they want us to support the package. So it was seen as a burden, an additional consultative body. And when the French Presidency pushed for it, they opposed it. The Commission said: no, no, no, this is too complicated. And frankly, they wanted to have this package

adopted very quickly and they didn't want to be slowed down by
something they didn't find essential.

(Interview 2)

However, unions faced a more general challenge in the 2008 debate on
the ETS. The subject of debate – emissions trading – did not make it
easier for the unions to become more widely heard in the EU. This was
a new area for the unions, which required expertise which they lacked,
and this proved a real challenge for them. The Secretary advisor at the
ETUC said that not many unionists in Europe really understood what
was at stake (Interview 2). According to the Secretary Advisor at the
ETUC, the ETUC had to make a compromise. It could have invested in
learning and bided its time with its position on the ETS. But in doing so
it would have deprived itself of influence on the debate. Alternatively,
it could have positioned itself within the debate but risked employees'
problems not being well represented. This was a dilemma, but the conviction that emission reductions should be made in Europe and globally was stronger. This conviction was widely shared among European
trade union organizations. In the end, even the Polish mining unions
expressed such opinions many times during our conversations – that
emission reductions had to be carried out.

However, the issue that has apparently not been discussed enough
within the ETUC was how to represent labour in European climate
politics. The important question was how to strike a balance between
taking responsibility as European citizens for emissions reduction
and the statutory obligation of trade union organizations to protect
the European workforce. How should a European labour organization tread a path between local employment concerns, regional EU-
level responsibilities for employment protection and global obligations
to reduce carbon dioxide emissions? Although my interviewee from
the National Commission of Solidarność in Gdańsk did not see any
contradictions in these goals, the mining and industry unions had difficulties understanding the position the ETUC adopted towards climate
action and its impact on employment. One of the union activists put it
this way:

> When you talk to people informally, you can hear from some
> members of the ETUC, e.g. Germans, that they think the ETUC
> behaves like yet another environmental NGO and not a trade
> union organization. They fight in the name of some general,
> global interests instead of dealing with the issues they should be
> dealing with – that is to defend their members, the working people.

We understand and agree that the natural environment should be protected, and that we have some international obligations. But if the ETUC does not feel well defending employees, maybe it should change its profile completely.

(Interview 3)

A similar criticism came from two European industry federations – the EMCEF and the EMF. I had a long conversation with an EMCEF official who had been involved in the debate on the ETS. He was also present in Katowice and had been in communication with the Polish and German unions with respect to the ETS Directive in 2008. He talked about the position of the ETUC with a dose of irony, calling it "yet another European environmental NGO" (Interview 4). According to him, the ETUC started to operate more and more within the field of environmental NGOs. For him, the problem was that "in the ETUC they were using the language of guys from the WWF rather than the language of industrial trade union organizations" (Interview 4). He complained that the ETUC was not willing to reflect in any way on the discussions and interests voiced within the EMCEF's organizational structures.

The EMCEF, along with other European industry federations such as the EMF, began to get closer to European employers' federations. This was institutionally facilitated through a sectoral social dialogue. Meanwhile, the ETUC established a partnership with environmental NGOs, with the aim of scaling up the voice of European labour. The ETUC has become a co-founder of the Spring Alliance, which comprises the European Environmental Bureau and the Social Platform. The Spring Alliance is a platform for addressing employment, environmental and social problems before each European Spring Summit. I asked an ETUC official why they needed cooperation with the environmental movement and what kinds of benefits this brought:

The environment is not an issue within our natural competence, so we need the environmental movement to be credible, to learn, to broaden our audience. Social movements are also very useful because they bring expertise and legitimacy on issues like energy poverty, housing, sustainable housing. So it really is an alliance you need when you say "sustainable development". We need to broaden our scope and we need to include other points of view, other issues. It was natural to cooperate with them. It never raised any difficulty within the ETUC. I'd say it is easier to work with NGOs, to a certain extent with those NGOs, than to work with business organizations.

We had experience within the European Partners for Environment, which brings together some companies, labour unions, NGOs, but it was not very successful and each time we tried to come to an agreement it failed, because it was impossible to have common ground with business organizations.

(Interview 2)

The debate on the ETS seems to have been a culmination of this organizational re-scaling of relations between the ETUC and industry federations within the wider field of European policy-making. At times, the language, concepts, loyalties, playing fields and feelings of urgency were so different between the ETUC and the federations that communication became a challenge. As my interviewee from the EMCEF pointed out, constructive discussions were difficult because each party was convinced that the other was fundamentally wrong. The ETUC thought that the EMCEF was making an error by allying itself with employers from particular sectors since they were supposed to be "the unions' natural enemies". The EMCEF thought that the ETUC was making an error by getting close to environmental NGOs because this suggested that it cared more for the environment than for the workers. At the same time, the European Commission was prioritising business needs over the needs of European labour. Carbon dioxide blurred the lines of the old alliances and oppositions. Industry workers' unions were ready to fight for better conditions together with their employers on the EU ETS. Service workers and leaders of the European Trade Union Confederation would rather ally themselves with environmental NGOs to strengthen their position vis-à-vis businesses and the European Commission. The playing field was different for national and industry union leaders and for EU-level union leaders. While the former had direct contact with workers, the latter were working with Brussels policy actors on a daily basis.

Shale gas politics and new terrains for state–citizen relations

In order to understand how relations between the Polish state and its citizens were negotiated within various terrains of the shale gas project, one needs to examine how these terrains were constructed. Despite a generally positive media discourse about shale gas in Poland (Wagner 2015, 2017), the Polish government feared that its own citizens might follow in the footsteps of anti-fracking groups, which were very vocal in countries such as France, Germany and Romania, and begin protest actions. In order to assess the situation, the government commissioned an opinion poll. The study by the Centre for Public Opinion Research (CBOS) in Warsaw showed a high level of support for shale gas exploration activities – 73 percent were in favour and only 4 percent wereagainst it (23 percent had no opinion on the issue). On a local level, support was also declared as being high. When people were asked about their attitudes towards operations in their neighbourhood, 56 percent were in favour and 21 percent were against it. These figures were encouraging for politicians and provided the government with an additional argument in favour of moving forward with fracking (Lis 2018).

A new terrain for negotiating shale gas development between citizens and state actors was established after the European Commission presented its recommendations for minimum standards for the exploration and exploitation of unconventional hydrocarbons on 22 January 2014. In October 2013, the Polish Ministry for the Environment developed a programme called "Let's Talk about Shale Gas"[1] in two regions where most of the exploration activities were taking place: in the Pomeranian Region (the northern part of Poland) and in the Lublin Region (the south-eastern part of Poland). The programme included two public hearings designed as open discussion forums where experts would answer questions from the audience. This rather unidirectional form of communication was proposed as a means of addressing the alleged knowledge deficit on shale gas widespread among Polish citizens – the usual diagnosis made by Polish politicians and experts whenever particular technological projects are not socially accepted (Lis and Stankiewicz 2017). As for many other similar communication processes organized by state institutions (e.g. the campaign for nuclear energy), experts fed the public technical information (expert knowledge) believing that in this way they would gain the citizens' trust and approval of the shale gas project. The main goals of the programme, as outlined by the Ministry, were to supply the public with reliable and comprehensive information about shale gas extraction and to create a space for dialogue between the various stakeholders.[2]

Various actors commissioned surveys on shale gas development in Poland, but if one takes a closer look, they all represented the state in one way or another: the Ministry of Environment, the state-owned oil and gas company PGNiG and the Polish Geological Institute (PGI) in Warsaw. Survey technologies were used to turn people's opinions into an objective representation of the Polish citizens' will (Lis 2018). This underscored governmental strategies and political discourse about the "positive impacts of shale gas exploration in Poland and Polish citizens' reasonable attitude towards it".[3] Perversely, a representative sample became a much more reliable and "real" interlocutor for some state officials than any group of concerned citizens that could be confronted in person (Lis 2018). Groups of complaining or protesting citizens were always seen as situated in a particular local context of interests, values and agendas, and therefore biased (Interview 5), while surveys seemed to have the quality of objectivity. In some sense, surveys enabled state institutions to do politics without citizens – without having to engage with them directly – unless a direct conflict occurred.

In 2012, the Marshall of the Pomeranian region established the office of the Plenipotentiary for Unconventional Hydrocarbons, which became responsible for communicating with stakeholders in the region (Lis 2018). Driven by this idea, a local NGO and a group of Polish sociologists designed a programme called "Together about shale gas", which proposed the creation of local negotiation groups composed of various stakeholders that would regularly meet to discuss matters of concern together with invited experts. As I point out in another publication (Lis 2018), the outcomes of the programme were supposed to benefit the participants, feed into the policy processes at the central level, and help to build an institutional order at different levels of administration. While the amount of information gathered during the meetings was impressive, the final recommendations prepared by the group members were sometimes inadequate for the existing institutional frameworks. These dialogue events were not attached to any "scaling machine", as, for example, in the case of the PGI reports and UH Network described in the previous chapter. The project was declared to be of interest to the National Fund for Environmental Protection and Water Management and the Ministry of the Environment. The Chief Country Geologist promised to take the recommendations into account. However, the discussion ended when oil and oil-indexed gas prices went down and companies began to withdraw. Seven reports, one from each group, are all that is left from the programme. As the Plenipotentiary pointed out, this knowledge was not consumed by the government, though the dialogue served as an exercise in and an opportunity for self-governance. It also resulted in a re-scaling of the discussion about energy from a central level to a regional one – after the programme ended, the Marshall's Office began to work on building "energy islands" with the aim of encouraging local governments to cooperate with companies and local communities to construct local intelligent energy solutions based on renewable energy sources and (conventional) gas in order to become less dependent on the central energy system (Lis 2018).

Yet another example of state–citizens interaction emerged through protest actions that took place in the Pomeranian region in the north of Poland, in the village of Przywidz (Cirocki 2011; Materka 2012;

Stasik 2017), and in the Lublin Region in the south-east of Poland, in the village of Żurawlów (Lis and Stasik 2018; Cantoni et al. 2018; Materka 2012). Near Żurawlów, the agricultural population "refused to sign consent forms, 'blocked' entire fields by building consensus among their neighbors, signed petitions, staged road blockages to stop company trucks, stole cables from drill rigs, rallied their local governmental (*gmina*) representatives to reject the exploration and use available public land for other investment purposes like building supermarkets" (Materka 2012, p. 19). The demographic of the protest group in Żurawlów was rather unusual – it was made up of farmers, city-based activists, anarchists, NGO representatives, MEPs from other EU member states and a French film-maker and his wife, who came up with a name for the protest (Occupy Chevron) and launched a protest website (Lis and Stasik 2018; Cantoni et al. 2018). As Agata Stasik recalled from her visit to Żurawlów in 2014 – to celebrate an international festival commemorating victory over the American shale gas developer Chevron – the event attracted many environmental and political activists from bigger cities. And it was mostly the city-dwellers that enjoyed dancing to the alternative punk and rock music played at the scene. The local youth stood around the playground looking a bit confused, feeling a bit out of place, not really having fun in their own village.[4] In an interview, an official from the Ministry of Foreign Affairs questioned "the reality" of the Żurawlów protest. He suggested that the main drive behind its organization was "neighbours' envy", as one landowner had leased his land to Chevron and others were unable to do so because their land was not part of the licensed area (Lis 2018). He also pointed out that the protest action was mainly carried out by people from outside the village – it was thus "not a real local protest" (Interview 5). In the eyes of the official, the heterogeneous composition and the non-local scale of the Occupy Chevron protest made it "less real", less valuable in terms of real local concerns, of dubious provenance and playing into the hands of various city-based activists, and even of foreign powers (Interview 5).

These publics constituted new terrains for negotiating state–citizen relations (Lis 2018). State politics around shale gas involved complex manoeuvring between different citizens to keep the shale gas project afloat. This involved making some publics visible and others invisible, scaling some up and downscaling others. While statistics from opinion polls were eagerly presented on various political forums (and in the EU), local protests were ignored or disregarded as not genuine or manipulated by foreign actors. Opinion poll results served to strengthen the government's discourse on shale gas and energy security presented by the Ministry of Foreign Affairs in Brussels. Within the EU arena, the

Ministry of Foreign Affairs, together with PGNiG and the other actors involved, presented the view that Polish citizens were largely in favour of the shale gas project (Lis 2018). They cited the opinion polls and proudly claimed that Polish citizens had not been influenced by the environmentalist hysteria and had, in general, acted reasonably (Interview 5). At the same time, the two main protest actions, in Przywidz and Żurawlów, had also come to the attention of governmental officials. However, they were perceived as exceptional cases, and the environmental, social and economic concerns expressed by the activists from Żurawlów and Przywidz were disregarded by high-level state officials (Interview 5).

While conducting interviews at the European Parliament in Brussels, I learned that anti-fracking protests in Poland were seen as rare exceptions or even disregarded as cases which involved strange, often psychologically unstable people (Interview 6). Local protests were seen as being generated not by the shale gas industry itself but rather by local conditions, contingent on the specifically local mix of actors (usually having strong relations to environmental NGOs outside of the local community) and sometimes as a result of companies' misbehaviour towards the local population. If a local protest does not have a transnational effect, it remains invisible to the European Commission, as a high-level official from the DG Environment pointed out to me in an interview (Interview 7). However, even if regarded as "exceptional, locally specific cases", the protests in the northern (and later on southern) parts of Poland did have some impact on the government's behaviour. The first attempt to make protest publics invisible came in the draft proposal of a new Geological and Mining Law (in force since 1 January 2012 but subsequently amended several times).

The new regulations proposed by the Polish government were aimed at accelerating exploration and making it easier to move on to the extraction phase. At the same time, the government tried to secure as much budget revenue as possible from future extraction, which was not welcomed by the companies involved (Lis and Stankiewicz 2017). However, the waste side of the project was not regulated, and this has concerned not just experts but also local communities that are directly exposed to the waste and have experienced its material presence on various occasions. During the exploration stage of the Polish shale gas project, most post-fracking waste had a signature "other". As long as very little post-fracking waste came to the surface, because only a few hydraulic fracturing operations were being carried out, their signature did not constitute a problem. However, the production phase would be much more intensive and would require managing and processing large quantities of waste – both solid and fluid. According to research carried out by the PGI, fluids coming back up to the surface contained a lot of salt and sometimes heavy metals and radioactive or other dangerous substances, depending on the type of rock through which the water would be passed through during the production process. After each fracturing operation, as the PGI experts explained to me, around 20–30 percent of the fracking fluid would come back to the surface. And while the composition of fluids used for fracking is fairly well known, as companies usually disclose this information to the public, the composition of the returning fluids has not yet been studied. There are also no regulations calling for any sort of chemical analysis. To a large extent, the fluid is recycled and used again (Interview 8).

Experts from the PGI were the first whistleblowers in regard to the impending waste challenge. As early as 2012, researchers from the PGI indicated in conversations with the Ministry of the Environment that waste management was likely to be the main challenge for the exploration phase (Interview 9). This conclusion was not written down in the report as, according to our interviewees, it was only a summary of the research results and it was not supposed to include any recommendations (Interview 9). The geologists recalled that before the public launch of the Łebień Report, the Ministry organized a number of meetings to discuss how convey the message to the general public that shale gas exploration was safe (Interview 9). When one of the experts I had interviewed delivered an extensive study on the environmental impacts of fracking to the Ministry of the Environment, she told the Minister about the approaching problem. The expert said that once the shale gas project entered the production phase, post-fracking waste would become a problem for the whole country. The Geological Department of the Ministry responded quickly and passed this information on to the Department of Waste Management. However, the report itself was filed away in the Minister's drawer. Only after some time had passed did journalists learn about it and bring the issue to light. One challenge resided in the difficulty of correctly classifying the post-fracking waste. It was not clear whether it would be classified as sewage or as waste, each of which would require a different purification procedure. The Ministry began thinking about how to deal with that the problem, but no concrete solutions were proposed. In the meantime, geological law was changed and the option of pumping post-fracking fluids into deep underground formations was eliminated. During the next round of amendments, this option returned to the text of the legislation.

The issue of waste disposal re-emerged in different contexts and in relation to different actors. Local stories about cases of illegal waste disposal by companies contracted by the project developers mushroomed both in the north and south of Poland. During a work-shop that I organized with my project partner Agata Stasik in Warsaw in May 2017, we asked civil society representatives as well as geologists about their experience of this issue. Activists told us that their main task was to constantly watch every step of the state administration and companies – waste management was particularly difficult to monitor. Post-fracking waste was difficult to trace, as public institutions did not keep track its progress from the producer to the waste processing plant. Waste could easily disappear; it was invisible to administrative bodies and civil society actors the moment it was taken from the pro-duction site as the "other" type of waste. Both the activists and the expert geologists were concerned about this. The problem of waste management was a clear sign of the weakness of the Polish state. Public institutions were unable to keep track of what companies did with the waste, and the Ministry refused to propose new regulations. This played into the hands of corporate interests, who wanted to get rid of the waste as swiftly and cheaply as possible. If the shale gas project ever returns to Poland, the waste issue may return and may mobilize the public against the industry. Imagery connected to waste, its toxicity and its imme-diate threat to human health may potentially have the greatest power to mobilize people against techno-scientific projects.

Conclusions

The 2008 debate on the ETS Directive has shown that trade union organizations in Europe are frustrated, but are trying to find the best strategy to represent the problems of labour with respect to the EU's cli-mate policies. In 2005, three trade union organizations, the International Confederation of Free Trade Unions (ICFTU), the European Trade Union Confederation (ETUC) and the Trade Union Advisory Committee (TUAC) to the Organisation for Economic Co-operation and Development (OECD), issued a common statement to 11th session of the Conference of the Parties of the United Nations Framework Convention on Climate Change (UNFCCC) in Montreal, Canada, on "Preventing Disruption & Enhancing Community Cohesion: Social & Employment Transition for Climate Change". Union organizations called for "green jobs" to be created, and for the establishment of re-employment, training and education programmes.

Since 2005, the concept of "green jobs" has systematically been refined within trade union forums and meetings. It has also started to bring together unions and governments. In March 2005 in the UK, a national GreenWorks (environmental) conference, addressed to trade unions from industry and public and private-sector services, was hosted by a joint government–trade union committee. The goal was to strengthen union workplaces and policy engagement in sustainable development, including energy and climate change. In 1998 the Trade Unions for Sustainable Development Advisory Committee (TUSDAC) was set up and is jointly chaired by a Government Minister and a Trade Union General Secretary. Spain provides another example of institutionalized dialogue on sustainable development and climate change between unions, the government and businesses. The problem of "green jobs" has been widely researched, not just by trade union organizations but also by environmental NGOssuch as the WWF. In 2009, the WWF published a report on low carbon jobs for Europe (WWF 2009). The report states that evidence to date suggests that green jobs span a wide array of occupations, skill levels and salaries, potentially offering opportunities for broad sections of the workforce. It makes it clear that some jobs will be lost while others will begained, but that this makes it difficult to foresee future scenarios for particular member states. This generates tension in the European labour movement. Knowledge on "green jobs" is produced mainly at the EU and international levels, while policy solutions are left to national governments.

At the Warsaw workshop in May 2017, which was organized by the author and her project partner, Agata Stasik, and aimed at summing up past experience with shale gas exploration in Poland, experts and activists were in agreement about the weaknesses of Polish state institutions. The institutional system, according to them, revealed a lack of robustness when it came to overseeing companies' activities, with waste management as a particularly weak spot. A lack of strong controlling agencies and poor communication between them made it difficult to sufficiently protect the environment and local communities. Regional environmental agencies were seen by workshop participants as not having enough power to properly regulate companies. The only institution that actually has the power to close down a mine is the Chief Mining Office and its regional agencies (Interview with expert geologist, 2017). Each company needs to report its daily activities to the Office, including any cases of accidents, spillages or broken containers. The Office has a right to carry out a control visit to the mine, and, in the event of violation of regulations, to close it. The strength of the Mining Office is a post-socialist legacy. Mining, especially coal mining, was an important part of the Polish economy during socialism and remains so today. Miners and mining unions constitute a strong political force, and institutions that operate around the mining sector are very powerful. The shale gas project, for the very first time, brought the

Mining Offices into closer cooperation with the Regional Directorate for Environmental Protection. They signed an agreement that they would inform each other about the activities of shale gas exploration companies on the ground (Interview with expert geologist, 2017). The vision of the Polish state shared by activists and expert geologists is bleak: "The companies basically were given the green light given by the state to do whatever they wanted", said one activist, and "they were allowed to ignore all regional and local institutions" (Interview with activist, 2017). The activists felt that the state institutions treated the companies much better than the citizens: "If I want to put up a garage, I need to have all my papers in order, but if a company does not have all the required documents, an official from the environmental agency would say: oh, it's ok, you can bring the missing documents later" (Interview with activist, 2017). Polish state institutions were basically seen by activists as agents of corporate interests: "The company wants to drive its trucks through the village but they are too heavy to do so legally. What do they do? They call the police and they come with the necessary permit. And off they go" (Interview with activist, 2017). The police, according to the activists, should be trained in environmental law. Environmental policing is what citizens would like to see in Poland.

Notes

1 http://lupki.mos.gov.pl/.
2 http://lupki.mos.gov.pl/o-kampanii/informacje-podstawowe
3 http://www.ekologia.pl/srodowisko/zrodla-energii/polacy-chca-gazu-lupkowego,16888.html
4 Stasik, participant observation, Żurawlów, June 2014.

References

Cantoni, R., Lis, A. and Stasik, A. (2018) Creating and debating energy citizenship: the case of Poland's shale gas. In: A. Szolucha (ed.), *Energy, Resource Extraction and Society: Impacts and Contested Futures*. New York: Routledge, pp. 53–69.
Lis, A. (2018) Politics and knowledge production: between securitization and riskification of the shale gas issue in Poland and Germany. In: K. Szulecki, (ed.), *Energy Security in Europe: Divergent Perceptions and Policy Challenges*. Cham: Palgrave Macmillan, pp. 93–116.
Lis, A. and Stankiewicz, P. (2017) Framing shale gas for policy-making in Poland. *Journal of Environmental Policy and Planning* 19(1): 53–71.
Lis, A. and Stasik, A. (2018) Unlikely allies against fracking networks of resistance against shale gas development in Poland. In: J. Whitton, M. Cotton, I.

M. Charnley-Parry, and K. Brasier (eds.), *Governing Shale Gas Development, Citizen Participation and Decision Making in the US, Canada, Australia and Europe*. London: Routledge, pp. 117–130.

Materka, E. (2012) Poland's quiet revolution: of shale gas exploration and its discontents in Pomerania. *Central European Journal of International and Security Studies* 6(1): 189–218.

Stasik, A. (2017) Global controversies in local settings: anti-fracking activism in the era of Web 2.0. *Journal of Risk Research* 21: 1562–1578.

Wagner, A. (2015) Shale gas: energy innovation in a (Non-)knowledge society: a press discourse analysis. *Science and Public Policy* 42(2): 273–286.

Wagner, A. (2017) Shale gas in the Polish media discourse. In: A. Wagner (ed.), *Visible and Invisible: Nuclear Energy, Shale Gas and Wind Power in the Polish Media Discourse*. Kraków: Jagiellonian University Press, pp. 125–153.

Documents

Directive 2009/29/EC of the European Parliament and the Council of 23 April 2009 amending Directive 2003/87/EC so as to improve and extend the greenhouse gas emission allowance trading scheme of the Community, in: Officlam Journal of the European Union, 5.6.2008.

EMCEF (2008) Position of the Coordination Office of EMCEF – Poland about the Climate Change and Energy Package, October 2008, Katowice: Coordination Council EMCEF, 7 October 2008.

ETUC (2008) ETUC's position on the Climate change and energy package, Position adopted by the Executive Committee of the ETUC at its meeting of 4 March in Brussels (EC. 179).

WWF (2009) Low Carbon Jobs for Europe: Current Opportunities and Future Prospects. Retrieved 10 July 2009 from http://greenjobs-ap.ilobkk.or.th/resources/low-carbon-jobs-for-europe-current-opportunities-and-future-prospects

Media report

Cirocki, B. (2011) Gmina Stężyca nie chce zysków z gazu łupkowego. *Dziennik Bałtycki* (11 November 2011). Retrieved 12 December 2011 from https://dziennikbaltycki.pl/gmina-stezyca-nie-chce-zyskow-z-gazu-lupkowego/ar/475615

Interviews

Interview with Activist, Workshop, Warsaw, May 2017.
Interview with Expert Geologist, Workshop, Warsaw, May 2017.
Interview 1: Expert at the EMCEF, Brussels, June 2009.
Interview 2: Expert at the ETUC, Brussels, April 2009.

Interview 3: Expert at the National Commission NSZZ Solidarność, Health and Safety Department, Gdańsk, November 2008.

Interview 4: Expert at the EMCEF, Brussels, March 2009.

Interview 5: Expert in the Ministry of Foreign Affairs, Warsaw, May 2015.

Interview 6: MEP's assistant, Brussels, June 2015.

Interview 7: DG Environment Official, Brussels, June 2015.

Interview 8: Expert at PGI, Warsaw, September 2015.

Interview 9: Expert at PGI, Warsaw, September 2015.

Conclusion
CEE countries and the challenge of knowledge production

The history of post-accession Poland discussed in this book is far from complete. I have only addressed the politics and expertise production surrounding the emergence of two items on Poland's energy policy agenda: carbon dioxide and shale gas. However, I would argue that in so doing I have told the story of some key moments of change in Poland's history. One way of recording transitions is to find pivotal moments when countries and their societies change their political or economic classification – for example, from authoritarianism to democracy, or from socialism to market economy – or when they change their civilizational identity, such as CEE countries becoming part of Europe again. Poland has had two such important moments in its recent history – in 1989 and 2004. These transitions were made publicly visible by different actors, including academics; they attracted significant attention and became objects of recurring re-interpretation by politicians. However, transitions do not only happen in this way. Within this book, I argue that profound transitions, though less celebrated and publicized, also occur due to the emergence of objects that demand new interpretation and re-organize relations between the different actors.

Carbon dioxide became such an object, some might even say an actor, in Poland's energy politics due to global and EU concerns about climate change, and as long as anthropogenic emissions of this greenhouse gas threaten the climate, carbon dioxide is not going to disappear from Poland's political and economic life. Accounting for carbon dioxide in energy generation will continue to change this sector for many years to come. Even if the current process of change has not yet brought a vast technological transformation, it will in the near future, as the 2019 increase in electricity prices in Poland shows. Shale gas, on the other hand, could have become a revolutionary object for Poland's economy. It had the potential to transform Poland's economy and its geopolitical relations with its current natural gas suppliers, such as Russia, in a relatively short timespan of several years. However, the difference between shale gas and carbon dioxide is that, while the latter is physically abundant in the Polish economy, the former needed to be physically introduced, and attempts to do so failed.

At the same time, the accounts given in this book remind us that the politics is inherent in the construction of markets, even if it is often hidden behind the veil of technicalities and black boxes, which makes market organization, to use Barry's (2001) expression, an exercise that is "profoundly anti-political in ... effects" (p. 270). During EU Green Week in May 2009, the European Commission presented the final text of the new ETS Directive as an economically and environmentally efficient solution. An official from the DG Environment said that changes introduced to the ETS Directive, proposed by the Commission in January 2008, were minor and this gave evidence to the fact that the initial proposal of the Commission was almost perfect. At that meeting, the rules of the ETS were discussed in terms of their efficiency, technical feasibility and accordance with European legal frameworks. This shows that to study the ETS as a political matter may at times be challenging and counterintuitive.

What and how to trade on the ETS raised many controversies in 2008. Frames and frame innovations were quite central to the process. For instance, framing of carbon dioxide as a commodity was challenged by Polish actors, and the interests of various actors were often re-framed in the course of the negotiation. The thesis illuminated processes through which the framing of "the economic" was often challenged by actors who pointed to extra-economic reasons such as fairness, solidarity and equality to enlarge the proposed frame. This also points to the fact that economic framing is selective because it cannot encompass everything. Framing implies leaving some parts of the reality outside. In this sense, frames are political and framing may be a coercive process; at the very least, it is never a power-neutral one. The performativity approach to the economy, despite numerous accusations (Miller 2002), may thus provide us with a means of accounting for power and politics. What stays inside and what stays outside a frame is never obvious or self-evident. It is always the proposal of an order, which is never neutral in its results. A focus on how actors negotiate these frames, how they justify them and how they enact them in the actual process of trading may be one way of bringing the political potential of the performativity approach forward. The focus on frames and the processes of framing pointed to the social movement-like character of how the Polish state and non-state actors worked with the EU to negotiate the role and place of carbon dioxide and shale gas in the EU. These were two moments of great mobilization and although it was a mobilization of powerful elite actors, unlike in the case of a traditionally examined social movement, persuasion and framing were some of their main tactics.

In both cases, I argue, a particular mix of scientific and economic expertise, as well as technological tinkering and political framing, were necessary for turning carbon dioxide and shale gas into energy objects. These processes involved negotiations of their visibility and invisibility, of their public appearance (Barry 2013) and their valuation (Callon and Muniesa 2005). Rather like being a nuclear object (Hetch 2014), being an energy object is contextual and depends on the configuration of relations that the object has been placed within. Nuclearity, Hetch (2014) argues, "is a *technopolitical* phenomenon that emerges from political and cultural configurations of technical and scientific things, from the social relations where knowledge is produced" (p. 15). Energy objects are also "becoming" in the social relations of knowledge production. Different types of expertise meet and are put into a conversation at various levels: at the policy level, in the context of communities' and companies' encounters, and at the corporate level. Different actors engage in negotiating the value of these objects for their own use. Being an energy object is not a fixed status; it differs depending on the configuration of the relations within which it has been placed.

It is useful to note that the materiality of the studied objects themselves set the conditions under which sociopolitical and economic realities are to be re-organized. On the one hand, there is no essence in the studied objects that would make them relevant or irrelevant for energy politics. They need scientists, politicians, experts, communities, technologies, business actors and civil society groups to frame them in relation to energy systems. Yet, on the other hand, their materiality sets conditions for their framing. For example, carbon dioxide cannot be burned or processed into another market product (at least not yet), but it can be stored in underground saline reservoirs. Shale gas and shale oil, on the other hand, set harsh conditions for their accessibility. For many years, shale rock had been regarded as inaccessible for exploitation. Only after US-based oil and gas companies had begun to experiment with various drilling and exploration technologies did it become possible to exploit natural gas and oil resources from shale rock as well. Once the technology for hydraulic fracturing started to spread across continents and large quantities of extracted unconventional hydrocarbons became visible on global markets, shale gas and oil became politically relevant as energy objects for many governments around the world.

Therefore, the stories that evolved around these two objects also provide an opportunity for reflecting on the position of the Polish state within broader European and global orders. The ontological status of both objects – being priced or not, being physically present or not – was an outcome of the ability of Polish actors to establish relations with other actors, in the EU and beyond. Important relations discussed in both stories include those involving international economic capital, global corporations, industry, oil and gas companies, and energy producers. The relation between foreign capital and the Polish state here was characterized by a dependency – the Polish state needed foreign capital in order to develop new energy policies for Poland. In the account I presented, this dependency was particularly visible in the area of expertise production about the economic and environmental implications of carbon dioxide emissions and shale gas exploration, both of which relied on the involvement of foreign capital. In the former case, expertise on the economic implications of different rules (of the EU ETS) was produced in cooperation with European industry and German power sector companies; in the latter case, expertise on the economic and environmental impacts of shale gas extraction was produced thanks to investments of foreign capital in the exploration of Poland's subsoil. Studying transformations through a history of specific objects reveals a wide variety of actors that make these histories – and these are not necessarily national states or governments.

Mitchell (2011) talks about a shift in political calculations made possible by a new resource. Likewise, carbon dioxide and shale gas made new modes of political calculations possible. Green jobs became weighted against dirty jobs, and green economies against coal-based economies; energy security acquired a new price tag and economic development was re-defined in relation to renewable energy sources. These new political calculations became the causes of new public disagreements. Different publics questioned many of these new categories –Polish trade unions have questioned the new categories of "green" jobs, while some Polish local communities have questioned their relations to shale gas, the local and state administrations, oil and gas companies, and the state's vision for Poland's energy future. Objects rarely appear individually; rather they tend to be linked with other objects, actors and issues, thereby creating new discursive spaces, new spaces for politics and new daily practices. This in turn takes public disagreements beyond the realm of state institutions, to be played out at different sites (Barry 2013) where many new actors and objects become visible: local communities, social media, renewable energy technologies and workers' organizations.

Due to their close connection with state politics, the energy objects I have studied have required that state actors define Poland's energy politics in a sharper way. It thus seems viable to ask whether we are observing the birth of resource nationalism in Poland, or whether the story is perhaps more complicated. Reductions in carbon dioxide have surely threatened the established power relations, in particular the dominant position of the mining and coal-based energy sectors in the Polish economic and political system. The coal empire, which had grown around a myriad of inter-related organizations and in close relation to state structures, involved trade unions, service companies and various political bodies (Gadowska 2002). These structures would have had to reconfigure, shrink considerably or cease to exist if the cost of carbon dioxide had had to be accounted for according to the European Commission's 2008 proposal. Conversely, shale gas promised resource independence, energy security and a stronger Polish presence on the geopolitical map of resource extraction, and perhaps even of resource export. However, attempts to turn Poland into a commodity frontier – "a frontier of appropriation" (Moore 2015; Tsing 2005) proved much more difficult to accomplish in the conditions of EU membership than some had initially imagined. The matrix of relations within which shale gas was valued as a resource in Poland was complex; it involved capital, expertise, and state and civil society actors – none of which could have produced the resource or valuated it on its own. Cooperation between the different parties was necessary.

At the same time, Polish state and business actors performed discourse not only on resource nationalism, energy security and sovereignty, but also on development in regard to both objects. Had Poland become part of the developed world with its accession to the EU, or was it still struggling to achieve economic development? The book shows that the EU accession did not completely re-classify the Polish economy into a developed one in the eyes of Polish actors themselves. Development discourse was still present in their visions of possible futures, whether evoked by foreign actors, such as the US Energy Information Agency, or coming from their own longings and inspirations. However, a vital question is whether development discourse could still work for the CEE region in the same way as it had before EU accession? Prior to EU accession, the CEE region was defined by both Western European and North American actors as a region in need of development –of economic and political re-ordering. However, once inside the EU club, the CEE region's development was influenced by the political priorities of the EU itself, mainly its environmental and climate protection agenda, but also by the EU's democratic values, liberal agendas and technocratic policy processes. Climate and environmental concerns have caused energy policy to cease being solely about energy. These new issues continue to supplant an economic framing, demanding the inclusion of new categories: environmental impacts, greenhouse gas emissions, human health. Meanwhile, the EU, as a regional organization which had already placed environmental and climate issues high on its agenda in the 1980s and 1990s, has generated overflows in relation to coal-based electricity production and shale gas extraction in Poland.

The focus on framing as a mechanism of mobilization also furthers our understanding of what "Europeanization" may stand for. The concept of Europeanization has been widely discussed in the literature, mainly among political scientists and scholars in public policy, legal studies and international relations. Initial concerns about the process of supranational institution-building and policy-making led to a proliferation of studies which examined the impacts of domestic conditions on the outcomes of these processes (Green-Cowles et al. 2000). Green-Cowles et al. (2000) refer to Europeanization as "the emergence and development at the European level of distinct structures of governance" (p. 3) ranging from political and legal to social institutions. The emphasis here is mainly on problem-solving, which formalizes interactions among actors, and on policy networks specializing in the creation of authoritative European rules (p. 3).

Soon however, with the increasing infiltration of European policies into the EU member states, the need for a thorough study of institutional change at the national level was expressed (see Héritier et al. 1996). According to Olsen (2002), at the beginning of 2000s Europeanization was most commonly used to describe the various ways in which the EU impacted on the member states. Europeanization was conceived of as a transfer of sovereignty to the EU level (Lawton 1999) and a process by which domestic policy areas were increasingly subjected to European policy-making (Börzel 1999). Ladrech (1994) emphasizes the processual aspects of this adaptation. According to him, Europeanization is an "incremental process re-orienting the direction and shape of politics to the degree that EC political and economic dynamics become part of the organization logic of national policy-making" (p. 69).

Interest in politics and policy-making went hand in hand with studies of rule-making and the transfer of institutional models from the EU to its Mmember states. Some scholars emphasized the persistence of domestic arrangements (van Waarden 1995), while others pointed to far-reaching adjustments at the national level (Schneider 2001). Yet another group set out to come up with efficient analytical tools and strategies to account for different constellations of European integration (Falkner et al. 2005; Knill and Lehmkuhl 1999). For instance, focusing on a dominant form of European policy-making, namely the EU regulatory policy, Knill and Lehmkuhl identified three main types of EU–member state relations: positive integration, negative integration and framing integration (Knill and Lehmkuhl 1999). The first focuses on a direct change taking place within domestic institutions in order to prescribe particular institutional models coming from EU polices. The second points to the changing domestic opportunity structure, within which actors and institutions compete for resources and power, and the third studies the change of beliefs and expectations of domestic actors towards policy processes. The third mechanism provides a shift from studying institutions and rules towards studying actors and cognitive structures that guide their actions.

Adaptation and a process of learning new "ways of doing things", at both institutional and individual levels, lies at the heart of Radaelli's (2000) concept of Europeanization. He defines it as a process of

> (a) construction, (b) diffusion and (c) institutionalisation of formal and informal rules, procedures, policy paradigms, styles, "ways of doing things" and shared beliefs and norms which are first defined and consolidated in the making of EU decisions and then incorporated in the logic of domestic discourses, identities, political structures and public policies.
>
> (p. 4)

This definition underscores the importance of "change in the logic of political behaviour", which takes place "through a process leading to the institutionalisation in the domestic political system (at the national and-or subnational levels) of discourses, cognitive maps, normative frameworks and styles coming from the EU" (Radaelli 2000, p. 4). Radaelli argues for studying cognitive and normative aspects, such as discourses on Europe, norms and values, political legitimacies, identities, paradigms, frames and narratives.

In the reviewed concepts of Europeanization, one may notice an insistence on a duality between "the domestic" and "the European". Even in the framework proposed by Radaelli (2000), it is emphasized that what is "constructed at the European level" may be further "adopted at the national level". I would like to dismantle this duality and bring in a more "flat" picture of the EU. First, I claim that "the European" is produced in various localities, and this is done not though a simple top-down diffusion but through a communicative iteration of interactions between various actors. A "European template" does not exist out there for the actors to be adopted in their domestic practices, but it is constructed by actors who imagine what the European might be, who expect the European to be something more or less specific and who refer to their past experience, discourses and objects which embody the EU to negotiate "a European way of doing things".

If we decide to take a legalistic rather than a sociological or anthropological view on Europeanization we may succeed in finding out which legal frameworks resulted from national and which from European legislative processes. But I find this doubtful. However, certainly "a European way of doing things" is not something that everyone can objectively find or would know where to look for it. The Europeanness cannot be discovered but it can be produced by actors and assembled from heterogenous and often accidental bits and pieces. It may with time become inscribed in material objects or institutions and mobilized each time a "European example" has to be given, but it undergoes a constant process of reshaping and enacting by various actors. There are also certain "agential peaks" (see MacKenzie et al. 2008) of Europeanness such as the European Commission, but the way in which they become and act European should be subjected to empirical investigation. As Kowalski (2007) points out, state power may be examined as fieldwork, as may the power of Europe: as work carried out in various locations, in various fields, and across them to produce an effect of the EU.

Framing is an important mechanism of this fieldwork. Actors construct the EU as an arena for their claim-making and propose framing the things they are doing in a "European" way. The EU becomes a reference point, which allows actors to express the similarities between them. They gauge their interests, analyse them and try to articulate commonalities as being European. They may also strategically use this frame to invite actors to re-think their interests and objectives. This is often an efficient strategy for mobilizing others for a common cause. Schlesinger (1992) noticed that interests tied to national identities have mainly been seen as a potential source of resistance to European integration and Europeanization in policy and institutional areas. However, some studies have shown new boundaries of solidarity being drawn within and among organized interests, which have not always followed national borders (Dolvik 1997; Macey 1998).

I argue that the mechanism for bringing about these new boundaries is "frame alignment" (see Snow et al. 1986), and the capacity to represent one's interests in the EU – to engage others in a dialogue, to be heard, listened to and followed –not only requires an understanding of political processes and an ability to gather the resources necessary for easier access to political decision-makers (e.g. personnel, new skills) (Pleines 2008), but also an ability to come up with frames that resonate among heterogeneous actors that are associated with the interests, concerns and values of actors from a variety of fields. In the social movement literature, the process conceptualized as "frame alignment" (Snow et al. 1986) is defined as "the linkage of individual and SMO [social movement organization] interpretative orientations, such that some set of individual interests, values and beliefs and SMO activities, goals, and ideology are congruent and complementary" (Snow et al. 1986, p. 464). Framing is thus a mechanism for linking things and people together by helping them to recognize similarities and opportunities. It is a mechanism for inviting them to shift their attention, activities, visions, objectives, identities and problems into new directions. It displaces them "closer to Europe".

By this approach the EU becomes an effect of the actor's practices which involves a lot of framing efforts. It may thus be understood through Mitchell's (1991) theorization of state-making as a structural effect. Mitchell (1991) asks the question, How real is the State? I would like to ask the question, How real is the EU? In his seminal text, Mitchell (1991) proposes speaking of the state as a structural effect as opposed to a realistic entity. According to Mitchell (1991), the state "should be examined not as an actual structure, but as powerful, metaphysical effect of practices that make such structures appear to exist" (p. 94). He concludes that "the boundary of the state is merely the effect of such arrangements and does not mark a real edge. It is not the border of an actual object" (Mitchell 1991, pp. 94–95). According to Mitchell (1991), the state boundary is not a distinct thing, but a result of material processes of boundary-making. These processes are spread throughout society and are located in various institutions, discourses, practices and objects. And the boundary work is boundary work as long as it is recognized and accepted by others.

As I have argued above, policy-making is not the only time when the EU is produced. It is produced in national government, in schools and during daily conversations. But there is also a range of actors that seem to specialize in the production of the EU. These are the various think tanks, NGOs, journalists, statisticians and academics who draw a boundary around themselves in order to tag their work as "scholarship on the EU". Following the proposition made by Eyal (2009), the practices of these actors constitute the work of producing the boundaries of the EU. Through their "fieldwork" (see Kowalski 2007), the EU becomes a sphere which can be imagined, referred to and mobilized, and which acts in a disciplinary and a powerful way on actors. They are important centres of calculation of the EU and the Europeanness which collect elements from various locations in order to assemble them anew and present them to the world as European, on the EU, for the EU or against the EU.

From this perspective, the EU is in fact "flat" and the levels of EU governance become various locations of practices through which the EU is produced as a structural effect. The research programme of Europeanization that emerges from these considerations is a programme that stems from an anthropological tradition of practice-oriented research and from the actor–network theory that urges us to follow actors and pay closer attention to the controversies in which they engage. It also allows us to see the sociotechnically constructed character of "doing things in a European way" instead of setting out with the assumption that such ways of doing things have an objective reality independent of the actors themselves. By this approach Europeanness is not an immutable mobile (see Latour 1987).

I would like to conclude this book with the observation that the two objects I have accounted for in this book are not the only ones worth studying. There are many more objects that can induce profound transformations in societies and in their economies and politics. These include new technologies such as electric vehicles (EVs), nuclear power, smartphones and blockchain technology. I argue that the transitions evoked by objects are often less obvious, less politicized and less celebrated, and thus publicly less visible; however, their impacts and their potential to change societies, cultures and politics – sometimes even political systems – are often enormous. Transformations such as the ones examined in this book are an important topic of investigation for social scientists, historians, sociologists and science and technology researchers. Oftentimes, transformations revolving around particular material objects can tell us more about the character of social change, the re-scaling of politics, the reconfiguration of actors' relations and geopolitical spaces, and new constellations of power than transformations marked by highly politicized shifts.

References

Barry, A. (2001) *Political Machines: Governing Technological Society*. London: The Athlone Press.

Barry, A. (2013) *Material Politics: Disputes Along the Pipeline*. Oxford: Wiley-Blackwell.

Börzel, T. (1999) Towards convergence in Europe? Institutional adaptation to Europeanization in Germany and Spain. *Journal of Common Market Studies* 37(4): 573–596.

Callon, M. (1998) An essay on framing and overflowing: economic externalities revisited by sociology. In: M. Callon (ed.), *The Laws of the Markets*. Oxford: Blackwell Publishers.

Callon, M. (2009) Civilizing markets: carbon trading between in vitro and in vivo experiments. *Accounting, Organizations and Society* 34(3–4): 535–548.

Callon, M. and Muniesa, F. (2005) Economic markets as calculative collective devices. *Organizational Studies* 26(8): 1229–1250.

Dolvik, J. E. (1997) *Redrawing Boundaries of Solidarity? ETUC, Social Dialogue and the Europeanization of Trade Unions in the 1990s*, Arena Report No. 5/ 97. Oslo: ARENA: FAFO.

Eyal, G. (2009) Spaces between fields. Retrieved 20 June 2018 from www.academia.edu/19534736/Spaces_between_Fields

Falkner, G., Treib, O., Hartlapp, M. and Leiber, S. (2005) *Complying with Europe: EU Harmonization and Soft Law in the Member States*. Cambridge: Cambridge University Press.

Gadowska, K. (2002) *Zjawisko klientelizmu polityczno-ekonomicznego. Systemowa analiza powiązań sieciowych na przykładzie przekształceń sektora górniczego w Polsce [Political-Economic Clientelism: The System Analysis of Network Relations on the Case of the Transformation of the Polish Mining Sector]*. Kraków: Wydawnictwo Uniwersytetu Jagiellońskiego.

Green-Cowles, M., Caporaso, J. and Risse, T. (eds.) (2000) *Transforming Europe: Europeanization and Domestic Change*. Ithaca, NY: Cornell University Press.

Héritier, A., Knill, C. and Mingers, S. (1996) *Ringing the Changes in Europe: Regulatory Competition and Redefinition of the State. Britain, France, Germany*. Berlin: Walter de Gruyter & Co.

Hetch, G. (2014) *Being Nuclear: Africans and the Global Uranium Trade*. Cambridge, MA: MIT Press.

Knill, C. and Lehmkuhl, D. (1999) How Europe matters: different mechanisms of Europeanization. *European Integration Online Papers* 3(7): 1–19.

Kowalski, A. (2007) State power as field work: culture and practice in the French survey of historic landmarks. In: R. Sennett and C. Calhoun (eds.), *Practicing Culture*. London: Routledge, pp. 82–104.

Ladrech, R. (1994) Europeanization of domestic politics and institutions: the case of France. *Journal of Common Market Studies* 32(1): 69–88.

Latour, B. (1987) *Science in Action: How to Follow Scientists and Engineers Through Society*. Cambridge, MA: Harvard University Press.

Lawton, T. (1999) Governing the skies: conditions for the Europeanisation of airline policy. *Journal of Public Policy* 19(1): 91–112.

Macey, S. (1998) The European Union and women's rights: from the Europeanization of national agendas to the nationalization of European agenda? *Journal of European Public Policy* 5(1): 131–152.

MacKenzie, D., Beunza, D. and Hardie, I. (2008) A price is a social thing: towards a material sociology of arbitrage. In: J. Beckert,, R. Diaz-Bone and H. Ganßmann (eds.), *Material Markets: How Economic Agents Are Constructed. Clarendon Lectures in Management Studies*. Oxford: Oxford University Press, pp. 85–109.

Miller, D. (2002) Turning Callon the right way up. *Economy and Society* 31(2): 218–233.

Mitchell, T. (1991) The limits of the state: beyond statist approaches and their critics. *American Political Science Review* 85(1): 77–96.

Mitchell, T. (2011) *Carbon Democracy: Political Power in the Age of Oil.* London: Verso.

Moore, J. W. (2015) *Capitalism in the Web of Life: Ecology and the Accumulation of Capital.* London: Verso.

Olsen, J. P. (2002) The many faces of Europeanization. *Journal of Common Market Studies* 40(5): 921–952.

Pleines, H. (2008) Trade unions from post-socialist member states in EU governance: an analytical framework. In: J. Kusznir and H. Pleines (eds.), *Trade Unions from Post-Socialist Member States in EU Governance.* Stuttgart: Ibidem Press, pp. 17–31.

Radaelli, C. (2000) Whither Europeanization? Concept stretching and substantive change. *European Integration Online Papers* (EIoP) 4(8): 1–28.

Radaelli, C. M. (2004) Europeanization: solution or problem? *European Integration Online Papers* 8(16): 1–23.

Schlesinger, P. (1992) "Europeanness" – a new cultural battlefield. *Innovation in Social Sciences Research* 5(2): 11–23.

Schneider, V. (2001) Europeanization and the redimensionalization of the public sector: telecommunications in Germany, France and Italy. In: J. Caporaso, M. Cowles and T. Risse (eds.), *Transforming Europe: Europeanization and Domestic Change.* Ithaca, NY: Cornell University Press.

Snow, D., Benford, R., Rochford, B. and Worden, S. (1986) Frame alignment processes, micromobilization, and movement participation. *American Sociological Review* 51(4): 464–481.

Tsing, A. L. (2005) *Friction: An Ethnography of Global Connection.* Princeton, NJ: Princeton University Press.

van Waarden (1995) National regulatory styles: a conceptual scheme and the institutional foundations of styles. In: B. Unger and F. van Waarden (eds.), *Convergence or Diversity? Internationalization and Economic Policy Response.* Aldershot: Edward Elgar, pp. 45–97.

Index

For Product Safety Concerns and Information please contact our EU
representative GPSR@taylorandfrancis.com
Taylor & Francis Verlag GmbH, Kaufingerstraße 24, 80331 München, Germany

www.ingramcontent.com/pod-product-compliance
Lightning Source LLC
Chambersburg PA
CBHW050534270326
41926CB00015B/3221